The COUNCIL OF THE SEVEN LIGHTS

George W. Van Tassel

SAUCERIAN PUBLISHER

ISBN:9781736731437

© 2021, Saucerian Publisher

Al rights reserved. No part of this publication maybe reproduced, translate, store in a retrieval system, or transmitted in any form or by any means, electronic, mechanical, photocopying, recording or otherwise, without prior written permision from the publisher.

George Van Tassel and the Integratron

Prologue

George Van Tassel was an American author and ufologist once claimed to have been in contact with an extraterrestrial from Venus. He was a controversial figure in the annals of ufology.

Van Tassel was born in Jefferson, Ohio in 1910, and grew up in a fairly prosperous middle-class family. He finished high school in the 10th grade and held a job at a small municipal airport near Cleveland; he also acquired a pilot's license. At age 20, he moved to California, where at first he worked as an automobile mechanic at a garage owned by an uncle. While pumping gas at the garage, he met Frank Critzer, an eccentric loner who claimed to be working a mine somewhere near Giant Rock, a 7-story boulder near Landers, California. Frank Critzer was a German immigrant trying to make a living in the desert as a prospector. During World War II, Critzer was under suspicion as a German spy and was killed during a police siege at the Rock in 1942. Upon receiving news of Critzer's death, Van Tassel applied for a lease of the small abandoned airport near Giant Rock from the Bureau of Land Management, and was eventually given a Federal Government contract to develop and maintain the airstrip.

Van Tassel was an accomplished aircraft mechanic and flight inspector who worked for various firms between 1930 and 1947 before retiring to the desert. In 1947, Van Tassel left Southern California's booming aerospace industry to live in the desert with his family. At first, he lived a simple existence in the rooms Frank Critzer had dug out under Giant Rock. Van Tassel eventually built a new home, a cafe, a gas station, a store, a small airstrip, and a ranch beside the Rock.

He rose to prominence as a key figure of interest in 1953 after claiming that he had been awoken one night by an alien from

Venus named Solgonda. The being allegedly invited him aboard its spacecraft where Van Tassel was telepathically gifted the plans for a device called the "Integratron" which was said to be capable of rejuvenating the human body.

Van Tassel began constructing the Integratron in 1954 in "an intersection of powerful geomagnetic forces that, when focused by the unique geometry of the building, will concentrate and amplify the energy required for cell rejuvenation". The construction costs were partly paid for by an annual series of successful UFO conventions, the Giant Rock Spacecraft Conventions, which continued for nearly 25 years. The main structure's construction was complete circa 1959, but Van Tassel continued to work on the device until his sudden death in 1978.

According to Van Tassel, the Integratron's workings rely on the generation of strong "intermittent magnetic fields" resulting in the generation of plasma in the form of a coronal discharge and negative air ionization inside the building. The Integratron is based on the Multiple Wave Oscillator invented by Georges Lakhovsky. The Multiple Wave Oscillator is a combination of a high voltage Tesla coil and a split-ring resonator that generates ultra wideband electromagnetic frequencies. Van Tassel speculated that electromagnetism affects biological cells, and believed that every biological cell has a unique resonant electromagnetic frequency. According to van Tassel, the generation of strong ultra wideband EMF by the Integratron "resonates" with the cell's frequency and "recharges" the cellular structure as if it were an electrical battery. Van Tassel claimed that human cells "rejuvenated" while inside the structure. Van Tassel also claimed the Integratron is intentionally constructed atop a powerful geomagnetic anomaly and its construction is entirely of non-ferromagnetic materials, the equivalent to a modern radome

Saucerian Publisher was founded with the mission of promoting books in Science Fiction. Our vision is to preserve the legacy of literary history by reprint editions of books which have already been exhausted or are difficult to obtain. Our goal is to help readers, educators and researchers by bringing back original publications that are difficult to find at reasonable price, while preserving the legacy of universal knowledge. This book is an authentic reproduction of the original printed text in shades of gray and may contain minor errors. Despite the fact that we have attempted to accurately maintain the integrity of the original work, the present reproduction may have minor errors beyond our control like: missing and blurred pages, poor pictures and markings. Because this book is culturally important, we have made available as part of our commitment to protect, preserve and promote knowledge in the world. 'This title was originally published in 1958.

In his book of 1958: *The Council of Seven Lights,* George van Tassel produced a compilation of communications describing a reality that many of us are not familiar with. Much of the information is complex and was not easily understood. The subject matters include the cycling of twelve densities, the progressed evolution of planets, and the connection between gravity and electricity. He takes the reader far beyond our atmosphere to give technical data on the lines of energy, the conditions of space. He describes polarity, its positive and negative aspects, and applies theory to fact so the reader can understand every point he makes.The beginning of all creation has the same meaning as the ending of all creation, for all things have always existed and always will exist. Everything anyone has ever been or will ever be, he is now. This is a truth often overlooked in man's search for understanding. He forgets God was all there was, and therefore all there is now or will ever be. Van Tassel writes that religion and science are the same thing, the only difference being that they are two opposite viewpoints. Just as a wall is a wall regardless of which side one stands on, so are science and religion, life itself. According to Van Tassel, the Bible is an accurate history of events repeating themselves in cycles. He says there are predictions referring to spaceships throughout the Bible, among them the prophecy tat there will be a day when the ships will come to take the people who are ready, leaving those who are not prepared to face the cataclysmic destruction inevitably approaching.

This book explains the vortices of the human body that are responsible for the reasons that certain individuals affect one so strongly on meeting, a violent, a strong attraction without apparent cause, and also explain a person's effect on each others. In The Council of Seven Lights, the reader will ind many absorbing facets of knowledge - new data on atmospheric conditions, further information about space ships, and for the searcher who desires more understanding of the greater pattern of life, a philosophy well worth studying.

Editor
Saucerian Publisher, 2021

TABLE OF CONTENTS

Chapter		Page
	INTRODUCTION	9
ONE	THE MISSING LINK	15
	Drawing 1	20
TWO	INVISIBLE GEARS	29
	Drawing 2	(Between 30 & 31)
THREE	THE SUNS OF GOD	43
	Drawing 3	45
FOUR	TRINITY OF INFINITY	62
FIVE	UNSEEN SCALES	71
	Drawing 4	72
SIX	THE ANGELS OF SPACE	80
SEVEN	PRODIGAL MOTHER	93
	Drawing 5	(Between 94 & 95)
	Drawing 6	(Between 100 & 101)
	Drawing 7	(Between 104 & 105)
EIGHT	METHUSELAH'S TOY	115
	Drawing 8	117
NINE	THE SWORD OF DAMOCLES	124
TEN	THE FALSE CHARIOT	135

INTRODUCTION

Para-psychology has proven that the transmission and reception of thought is possible and a scientific fact.

The information in this book is the result of a developed ability to awaken the nearly dormant consciousness to thoughts existing throughout time.

Nothing can be thought of that has not been thought of before. The principles of radio, television, electricity, flying, and of all modern things, existed in the time of Plato and Columbus. All of the principles of everything that can ever be already exist in the infinity of Universal Mind.

The ability to penetrate Mind requires practice. In practicing the act of awareness I found that Intelligence exists throughout the Universe.

My first contact with the organized Intelligences of other places revealed that the Intelligence manifested on the Earth is in the kindergarten stages. My penetration into the superconscious mind revealed an eternal record of infinite laws.

Thinking is not something one does. Thinking is the act of becoming aware of what already exists. One does not try to think to become aware. One only has to remove his own thoughts and then the Universal Mind rushes in to fill the void.

The introduction of any new thought is usually accepted by those who understand its potentialities, and rejected by those who do not comprehend its

INTRODUCTION

portent. This often leads to controversy, which is the needed stimulant that brings individuals to the use of their own thought power.

This book is not written with the intention to present anything radically new to the reader. It is written to revive that which has become nearly dormant within his individual power of conception.

One would be utterly foolish to try to explain a subject using scientific explanations to another who is not interested in or doesn't understand scientific terms. It would be equally unimpressive to appeal to one from the religious viewpoint if he were not interested in religion.

My desire in presenting this book is to pass on that which makes sense to my reasoning faculties, in the hope that others can gain something of lasting value from it.

The materialism of the present society of the masses is evidence that even the most unreligious of individuals has a desire to worship something; so he worships matter. The materialists think they are the more advanced people in an otherwise scientifically ignorant society.

The most devout religionists lean the other way and believe their heavenly point of view is the correct way. Actually both are wrong and both are right; from a neutral point of view.

I am attempting to present this book from the middle viewpoint. If it appears that I am leaning one way or the other, the reader may take into account that perhaps he is basing his opinion on his

INTRODUCTION

own tendency to lean one way or the other. Now, the best way to really understand anything is to examine your own opinion from the *opposite* point of view.

This book is an attempt to present to science and religion the facts that each are integral parts of the other, and both are the same ONE from opposite concepts. A wall is a wall regardless of from which side one looks at it. On one side of this wall is written the history and achievements of science, and on the other side one can read the records of the various religions.

There is only the one principle of creation, but there are many roads to finding this grand principle.

Religion presents its *many* roads to the people; each sect presenting its approach as the *only* one, with the fanatic condemnation of all other religious roads. The many divisions of science each profess their findings as the eternal verities.

Religion presents God as the Infinite Being; and science presents the manifestations of God which have been recorded with the five senses.

In the unthinkable vastness of the infinite universe the Earth is only a tiny speck of matter, inhabited by parasites called humans. The people depend upon the Earth for their sustenance the same as any parasite depends upon its host for life.

Religion is the art of *living* now. A true religionist knows how to live without infringing upon the rightful living of others. The professors of religion pro-

INTRODUCTION

pound spirit as something you become after your death. Actually the spirit of you is here now and your god is determined by the way you live in the flesh body so as to manifest spirit now, here on Earth.

The consciousness of every individual contains all of the records of every act and personality that the individual has ever done, or been.

To admit that many of the thoughts I received were given by other identities would be true. Yet the further truth is that I have been all of these other identities.

Reincarnation is a misnomer. All that one has ever been or will ever be, he is *now*. Everyone has always existed since the creation.

Whether one accepts the limits of one life span here on the Earth, or this life and a hereafter somewhere else is of no concern. One cannot honestly believe in a hereafter without believing in a "before". This schoolroom on the Earth is only a brief experience in eternal Life.

One must first understand himself, then he may understand his fellowman. If this is accomplished then one is at the doorway of understanding God.

THE COUNCIL OF SEVEN LIGHTS

O man, you have made laws to avoid using My Laws.

Confusion, chaos, and war are the results of man's ideas, opinion, and assumptions.

Light alone is the essence of Truth;
Truth alone is the essence of Wisdom;
Wisdom is the essence of Knowledge;
Knowledge is the essence of Life.

Only through Knowledge can man express Wisdom in action.

I have given man Life that he might demonstrate My Knowledge through action and Wisdom.

I extend the concentration of My Light to those who are demonstrating My Laws.

O man, in living My life, in breathing My breath, establish within yourself the solidarity, the contentment, the bliss of living rightly; that I may know, that I may feel the glorious pulsation of the Being of you. In speaking My words, let them ring clear, let them be dear and near to you that others may understand. Realize, I am not the expression of self; I am only the boundless unselfish utterances of the heart and the Soul that sees Me in others. None can bring about the workings of My Laws, unless first they have established their right within My Light.

Reach not for golden prizes of desire, for they shall reflect the Light. Look not into the mirrors of space, for eyes that see are blind to Me. And though the prize be golden, My light does not reflect. Express the Being of Me in life, extend Me in the action that I may feel the thrill of doing for another whose need is great, that I may know success in manifesting you to bring about the Me in others, that their eyes may see through thee to Me—not reflection, not illusion, but the purity, the reality I have instilled within the you of Me.

CHAPTER ONE

THE MISSING LINK

"In the beginning God created the heaven and the earth." (Gen. 1:1). This creation was a part of the continuously evolving creation throughout the universe. Each instant that passes new things are being made, new phases of life unfold, to live in ever progressing cycles of rebirth.

As related above God made heaven before Earth. In these heavens of the sky He had already created Man. On many planets in many other solar systems, and on other planets in this solar system, Man was developed through thousands of years, even before the Earth was habitable.

Man was created (Gen. 1:27), *he did not evolve from the lower animals.*

However, he was not created on the Earth. Man was created throughout millions of solar systems; to serve as the instrument of God's doing. Anyone who contends that this planet is the only one occupied by intelligent life forms, does not accept God in His infinite completeness. His narrow mind has placed a limit on His ability to perform His creations.

Adam was not a single man. The Adamic *race of Man* was the first people to inhabit the Earth. This is confirmed in Gen. 1:27 where the race of Man, in the original creation, is described as "male and female". In Gen. 1:28 the scripture relates how "God blessed them". This is plural, not *him*, but *them*. And God said unto *them* (the Adamic race, both male and female) "be fruitful, and multiply". This all happens before Eve is ever mentioned. Thus the Adamic race is established on Earth.

Then God finished His work of creation in regard to Man. He had also finished the creation of the *heavens* and the *Earth* (Gen. 2:1) and all the host of *them*. This means all the beings who occupied the Earth and the *heavens*. So God "ended His work" and rested. (Gen. 2:2,3).

Can this be that God ended His work, and still no mention of Eve? Yes, the Bible is accurate on God's beginning of His creations.

Then comes the *summary* of the creation. This is where people are led into confusion. For the first time God is left out of the picture and we have a "Lord God" (Heb.-Jehovah Elohim). This *character* was one of the Adamic race who was in the colony that had been landed here by spacecraft. The men of the Adamic race did not bring their women with them when they first landed on Earth.

The Lord God brings Eve into the picture, not the Creator. The Lord God said that the Adamic men were lonesome. (Gen. 2:18). Then the Lord God pops Eve out of a rib after one of their people fell into a deep sleep. (Gen. 2:21,22). God brings about the creation of people through birth everywhere in the universe, not by making women out of men's ribs.

THE MISSING LINK

The *race* of Eve was the highest form of lower animal life on this planet. *They were not apes,* but they were also not the race of Man, *created by God.*

Next comes the story of Adam, Eve, and the apple. (Gen. 3:1-7). This son of the Adamic race of Man blamed the woman, and the woman blamed the serpent. The poor serpent didn't have anyone to blame.

One of the true species of Man, as God *created* the Adamic race, mated with an animal. There is no violation of God's law in man mating with woman *after his own kind.* Adam's violation of the law was not in "eating the apple"; it was in eating the *wrong* apple.

God created every creature after its own kind (Gen. 1:11,12 and 21, 22), but one of the race of Man mated with an animal of the Earth and *crossed blood.*

This is where Man became *hu-man.* Eve gave birth to Cain and Abel. She didn't know who the Creator was, so she said, "I have gotten a man from the Lord" (Gen. 4:1), thinking the Lord was the Adamic man who was her mate.

When Cain killed Abel he revealed the animal nature of his mother. He started the practice of murder, that has expanded to a point now where people can vaporize thousands of others with atomic and hydrogen bombs. That is why the people of the Earth are called humans. The Adamic sons of God knew the tiger as a killer among beasts. The name for tiger was "Hu".

THE COUNCIL OF SEVEN LIGHTS

Most of the people on the Earth today are crossbreed descendants of the true Adamic sons of God, as originally created, and the animal race of Eve. That is why you have an earthly, dense, animal body, and an inner body of created reality as God made *You*.

The truly created men and women of the Adamic race of man have been watching the people on the Earth for thousands of years.

This "siva-lization" (from Shiva, Hindu god of destruction) of humans has expanded the science of destruction to the point of crisis. The nations having atomic bombs have enough to wipe out all living things on the Earth. The animal of Eve is in power.

The Adamic race of Man has brought "nullifier" ships into the Earth's thin film of breathable atmosphere. We call them *green fireballs*. They have nullified concentrations of atomic radiation that were in our atmosphere. They feel responsible for the fact that one of their people started this destructive cycle on the Earth. You have a choice to make. You either accept the Creator's Adamic constructive part of you, or you recognize the physical *hu*-man's destructive influence of the Eve ancestry.

The Adamic race of Man typifies the combination of spirit and substance into form. The many *forms* of life; fish, birds, reptiles, insects, animals, and humans all change with environment and breeding. The human race is a degenerate species of Man, as a result of following the bestial tendencies.

THE MISSING LINK

Matter and spirit are the same thing, only in opposite manifestation. Matter is energy (spirit) condensed and energy is matter in solution. Each is polarized throughout infinite space and both follow a pattern of forms.

Space is the infinite ocean of Intelligence (Creative Spirit), or the Creator at rest. This balanced Intelligence manifests through all creations. In order to manifest *motion* the *energies* must be unbalanced.

No thing or condition in God's universe is without contrast in duality. For every up there's a down, for every white there's a black, for every night there's a day.

Anyone who has climbed the "tree of knowledge" can see that it has two sides, no matter in which direction one looks. This is not because the tree knows one side from another; it's because the man in the top of it has two sides, his right and left.

God made everything in duality so He could remain at rest in the middle. God is peace.

Jesus said "My Father and I are one". That was because he recognized no rich or poor, no boundaries or colors, no church or religions. That was because he remained neutral at a division point between the contrasting dualities. Jesus didn't take sides with anyone. Actually *you* shouldn't take either side—take God's course down the middle.

A fire can warm you or destroy you. Cold is desirable in a refrigerator but not when it makes one uncomfortable. Speed is required to get somewhere fast, but its momentum can kill you if you lose control of it.

Atomic energy is a death force. Its radiation can kill you without a bomb being dropped. In commercial use for power it is as deadly as when it is used in bombs.

Fission or fusion of atoms, or their isotopes, on a planet are not as God intended. God created suns to operate their reactions by the principles of fission and fusion. He also placed the planets far enough away from the suns so there would be no harmful effects from their waste products.

Human use of sun principles, on a planet, is in direct opposition to the creative principles of an all wise God.

The law of reaction will cancel every destructive cause. Apply sun principles on planets and the reaction will make the planet a sun. Who escapes? Only the people who are with God in the middle. How? They will be taken out into space by the race of Man in the spacecraft.

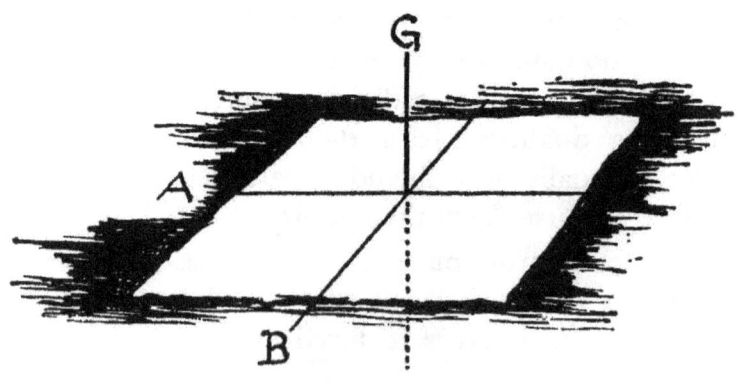

THE MISSING LINK

In order to present the one principle which causes all things to be, let us use the symbol "G" to signify what is commonly referred to as God. Let us use "A" to symbolize the right hand of God, or the positive polarity, projective, male force of unbalanced energy. Let us use "B" as the sign of negative polarity, receptive, female energy, or the left hand of God.

Assume that God, who rested after the creation of all things, is the still fulcrum of Intelligence throughout all infinity that serves as the balance between these opposites.

For an objective point of view, assume that the "G" line is vertical to the plane of the paper.

Assume that the "A" line is on the paper, running crosswise at 90° to the vertical "G" line. This "A" line of force is composed of positively charged particles.

Assume that the "B" line is running from the top to the bottom of the paper, at 90° to the "A" line and 90° to the "G" line. This "B" line of force is composed of negatively charged particles.

Where these lines cross there is an atom, a micro solar system, created in perfection by these unseen forces. The atomic element is determined by the substances present in the charged "A" and "B" lines. This evolves a nucleus of positively charged particles called a proton, surrounded by a field of negative orbits set up by the "B" particles in motion. The concentrated group of "B" particles in this orbit we call an electron.

The "G" line has no motion as to movement in a given direction. It extends infinitely throughout all space, through all substances and materials. It exists in what we term both light and darkness. These lines are parallel to each other.

Atoms compose all things. "G" light is found in the composition of all atoms. "G" light *is* Creative Intelligence.

Our Earth is an electron of our Sun, traveling in its orbit of a negative field. It is rotated by the band width of "A" and "B" light forces, equal to the Earth's diameter.

Prior to the formation of individual atoms, the "A" and "B" lines of light force had to contain the correct amount of substance particles.

For clarification let us revert down to a single line of "A" and "B" lines of force.

These two lines of oppositely charged light cross each other at 90°, insulated by the "G" lines of infinite Intelligence. They cannot be brought into induction where they cross unless they are mated.

In order to give birth to an atom of Hydrogen, the "A" and "B" lines must conform to species. The law reads "each after its own kind". The "B" must contain the same number of particles per inch as the "A" does. These particles must also vibrate at the same frequency.

In order to become Hydrogen both lines of light must conform to the vibratory frequency of Hydrogen in the spectrum. The vibratory frequency of each element is different. The Hydrogen particles vibrating in their own frequency in the light lines before they become an atom cannot mix with the frequency of any other element.

This makes them of like species in every respect except they are of opposite polarity. This opposition of charge brings them together, and the "G" light allows them to mate by induction because they are equal opposites.

The density of each element is determined by the frequency of the vibrating particles in both the "A" and "B" lines of force.

Each atomic element is the result of perfect proportion, charge, and vibration in equal and opposite polarities. Thus an atom of Hydrogen is the same wherever it is found in the universe.

Let us proceed to simplify the complex. Picture an onion cut in two. An onion is like an atom, the outside layer or shell being the negative field of orbit for the outermost electron. The next layer and each alternate layer toward the center being composed of Intelligence, the insulating layer of infinite light force called the "G" line of light. When you crack an atom, the force disturbing or puncturing the outer shell creates unbalance and neutralizes the outer shell. This causes the outermost electron to be attracted to the positive proton in the center. However, before the electron reaches the proton the instantaneous inrush of "G" light force through the fractured outer shell creates implosive pressures within the atom. This is the active force that brings about the explosion when the electron and proton discharge within the ruptured shell. The insulating "G" light condenses into what science has named a neutrino. This potent causation force immediately deserts its wrecked atom and takes off to return to the thirteenth density. This is what religion would term a "resurrection"; when the potent, causal, infinite, light force deserts its shell or body.

God in His infinite Wisdom caused all of His creations to function by perpetual motion. He maintains the balance by centering each creation and insulating each one from all others.

When He created the "A" lines of light force, He caused to be 1850 of them to a square centimeter. He gave them positive polarity, male, projective gender, a speed of 186,000 miles per second, and matter in the form of charged particles.

In opposition to the "A" lines of light force He created the "B" lines. The "B" lines are 1257 per square centimeter. They cross between the "A" lines of force at 90° with a speed of 202,000 miles per second. Their polarity is negative, their gender is female, receptive.

Between the "breathing" of these two primary forces, He created rhythm. This brings about a "wave motion", which consolidates the individual lines into "bands". When "A" works inward, "B" works forward; and when "A" works outward, "B" works backward. Rhythm, which establishes the "bands, levels, and density changes", is operated by strain or desire. Strain is the time between the "flight" of the female, negative lines of force and

THE MISSING LINK

"the pursuit" of the male, positive lines of force. When they encounter any created object that was "born" before by other "A" and "B" lines of light, they add to its rotation by spiral induction and partial penetration.

The negative "B" lines are attracted to the Earth's positive core, but are resisted by the "G" light insulation strata. Having penetrated the negative crust, they are repelled by it and take the line of least resistance, which is out of the North Pole. By induction, they attracted the positive core to rotate in one direction, and in being repelled helped the negative crust to rotate in the opposite direction. The "A" positive lines of force work opposite to the foregoing, and are emitted at the South Pole. As they emit from the poles they are met by the "A" and "B" lines of light that are passing uninterrupted by the planet and bent back to their original course. The resistance in bending causes the aurora.

As they have reduced their energy charge and speed of motion in adding power to the planet, they enter different levels as they emerge from the poles. Then the "G" lines of light, crossing between them and insulating them, brings them back through "rest" and "rhythmic breathing" to their original conditions.

The "A" lines of force have more quantity "density" and less speed than the "B" lines of force. The "B" lines have more speed and less "density". This is the reason why the "A" positive lines of force, charged with matter, become the proton core of the Earth. The faster "B" charged matter becomes the crust of our planet. This strain or desire is the eternal progressive spirit in all things that manifest action.

Strain in people is called desire. When the desire exceeds the limits of capacity, the Father's agents of balance—the "A" or "B" lines of force—will bring about an opposite result. The "G", "A", and "B" lines are the "Us" referred to in the Bible (Gen. 1:26) when God said, "Let *us* make man".

THE COUNCIL OF SEVEN LIGHTS

O mortals, though My Laws have been as doormats beneath your feet; though through centuries you have turned not to face the Light—I judge not, neither do I hold regrets, for all are given right to choose. Mortals in this density of three, having not chosen Me, now stand beneath the whip, but are rather facing rebound of the actions man has created. My Laws are fixed. None can change the Law of all Infinity. One fulfills the Law, or faces judgment by the Law, written in the Light of each of My created beings. Having turned My Laws about, now you are faced with your man creations in opposition to My Law. So I gather up the scattered fruit, knowing that the bulk of My harvest has been lost to repetition upon repetition of errors, written in the history of mortals on this portion of Me. I must brush off this contamination from My cloak, that I may hang it in My closet clean. Those who have failed for centuries to recognize My person within their Being, are forced by their actions to repetition once again. My heart, manifested by you, is sore. But I shall recover to bring about the destiny as many times as necessary, that My pattern shall be complete for each one of My parts. So it is, again and again I cleanse My house. My love shall never fail. Everlasting Light is man's by choice alone, and the choice I gave to him.

I am the voice that manifests in every word you say. I am the sound in darkness to your ear, that leads the way.

You stumble on the path to Me. You fail to see

the Light within, that grows with every victory over self.

To be a part of Me, project the actions of Me being you. Extend My Love instilled within. Do unto others as I do to you.

For I can only Be, through you.

CHAPTER TWO

INVISIBLE GEARS

Densities are the levels or grades through which creation progresses. Thought is the activating force. Thought is the image of the Creative Intelligence. Progression is a reward for effort expended in creative thought. Through thought the Creator established a pattern through which all things must pass.

The people of the Earth and this solar system are all in the same boat at present. There are various levels or decks in this space boat. There are visible partitions between these different levels.

The first class passengers in this solar boat are not the wealthy people, nor the intellectuals of the system. The steerage is not occupied by the poor or the illiterate. Everything in this boat is mixed up. The Creator didn't make it this way, the mix-up is due to the doings of man.

Earth people are dominated by individual and mass ego. Nearly everyone thinks he is better than others. Now progression is upward, and when one looks down on another he must lower himself to see the other. When one sees the good in others he automatically raises himself.

The Creator established densities to control these conditions. The Third density, where these things exist in the triangle of confusion, is about all finished. Humans on Earth are going to have to conform to the requirements of the Fourth density, or take this grade over again.

The requirement to pass is to *live* the Golden Rule. Not to profess it, or expect others to live it, but to live it individually, as you are only responsible for yourself.

The drawing represents one of the "flowers of the universe". The Vela Sector System is only one of the Creator's thoughts.

There are twelve densities in the system we occupy. Each of these is divided into twelve major cycles. Each major cycle is divided into twelve minor cycles. When a solar system moves out of one density into another, it is called a master cycle.

The solar system that we are in is now in the arc between the Third and Fourth densities. For the planet Earth and this solar system, this is the time of times. The Earth is culminating a minor cycle, a major cycle, and a master cycle all at the same time. This will bring about a rebalancing of the planet on new poles. When this occurs, the great earthquake written of in Revelations will take place.

The First density, for the Earth, was when the planet only supported vegetation. The Earth's rotational speed was such that only gigantic vegetation with a germination temperature of around 110 degrees Fahrenheit could survive.

When the Earth passed through the arc, or overlap between the First and Second densities, it rebalanced on new poles; and the massive vegetation became our coal beds of today.

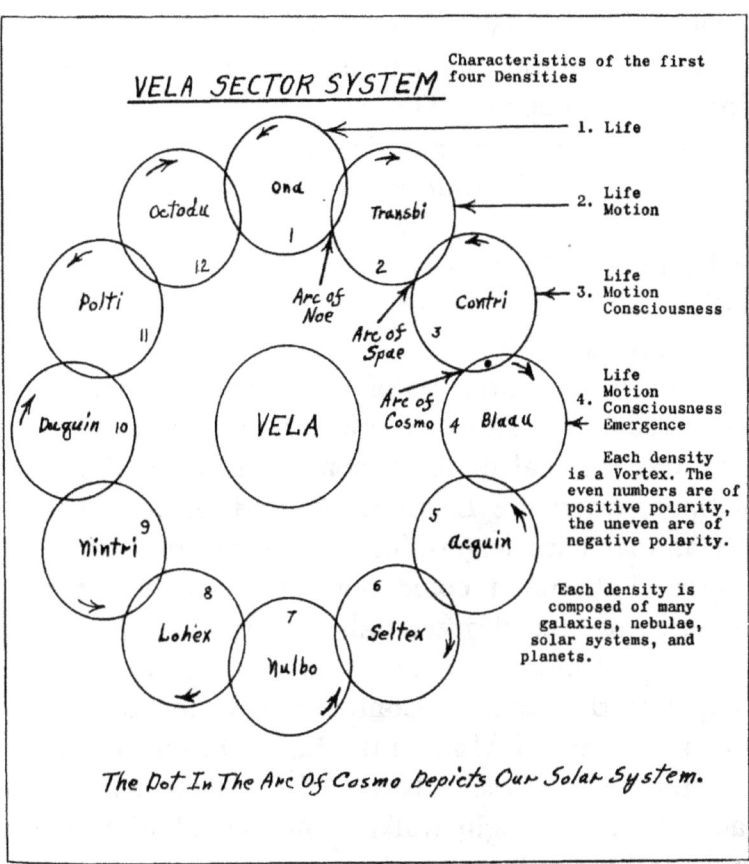

The Dot In The Arc Of Cosmo Depicts Our Solar System.

As soon as the Earth had stabilized in the Second density, the space people landed animals on the planet. This has been handed down from the ancient records as the story of Noah and the Ark.

The germination temperature in the Second density was 104 degrees. The animals that lived in the Second density were also large. They were of the mastodon and dinosaur types. The reason they became extinct when the planet passed from the Second into the Third density, was because the germination temperature in the Third density was around 98.6 degrees Fahrenheit.

Many of the carcasses of these large animals are recovered today from the glaciers of Siberia. That area was tropical in the Second density. In the arc of Spae, when the Earth rebalanced on new poles, the animal with a germination temperature of 104 degrees Fahrenheit could not reproduce in a temperature of 98.6 degrees Fahrenheit.

After the large animals became extinct the space people of the Adamic Confederation landed a colony of the race of Man on the Earth. It was through the mating of these Adamic Man people with the race of Eve (upright-walking animals of high Second density development that survived the cataclysm in the arc of Spae) that brought about the humans of the Earth. This was the beginning of human people in the Third density, on the Earth. The race of Eve became extinct, except for the animal flesh contribution and destructive tendencies of humans.

Humans cannot reproduce in the Fourth density

and will become extinct as an animal-Man mergence in the first 100 years, as the Fourth density germination temperature will be around 90 degrees Fahrenheit. The humans that survive through the cataclysm of the coming polar flip will gradually die off. The Fourth density is not for destructive principles or humans. Those who do not conform to the requirements to emerge will be reincarnated back into the 12th phase of the Third density on another planet, and have to live through this mess again.

The densities alternate polarity and therefore rotation. The drawing shows them as viewed from the top, looking at their maximum circumference. An edgewise view would show them as spirals, one with the apex up and the next with the apex down.

Our solar system is about to pass out of the maximum circumference of the Third density into the minimum circumference of the Fourth density. The Earth will then rotate nearly 370 days in a year.

Do not confuse densities with dimensions. Densities are pressures established in changing frequencies of vibration. Dimensions are measurements.

Some have mixed-up dimension and density. Time is not measurable in the Absolute. Time can be phased in density and moved backward or forward. However it can only be done through the zero point between polarities.

As our solar system moves through space, its progression is into an ever increasing frequency of vibrations. Each solar system and every planet must evolve through grades, even as babies learn to crawl before they walk.

The "A" and "B" lines of force pass through your body at 90° to each other. The "G" line of infinite light centers your consciousness and separates you from all other people with a boundary of skin. As these positive and negative lines of energy pass through your body, they activate every atom and cell of your physical makeup.

If the approach of these lines to this planet, from out of space, is interrupted by one of the other planets, as they are, then you individually are affected by the influence from the other planets.

Our scientists say the Moon causes tides, yet they contend that the Moon has no effect on crops, people, or other conditions, that these beliefs are only superstition. The human body is over two-thirds water. Is it superstition to assume that if the influence of the Moon moves thousands of millions of tons of water in the oceans, that the hundred pounds or so of water in a person is not also affected?

Everything has some effect on everything else in the universe.

As you move throughout the day in an upright position, you are moving in and out of many lines of force. All of them are charged with influences, not only of other planets but from other people, various metallic objects, electronic devices, and atmospheric conditions. You feel these influences and you may wonder how the day, or year, went so fast. At another time the hours may drag. These time changes are the results of some influence acting upon you.

If you work hard or run you become heated and tired. This is the result of an increase in the number of charged lines of force you have interrupted.

Through various attitudes caused by turning, bending, and motions of the limbs, heat is generated in the body because of constant changes of the "angle of attack" from the lines of force.

When you sit down to rest for a few minutes, this permits the body to absorb the energy from the "A" and "B" lines of force issuing forth from the same *unchanging* direction. Then the structure of the body cools off because it reaches balance. This idling condition of the body-motor is brought about by the fact that each atom is receiving steady motion by the same lines of force.

When you sleep at night the body becomes charged in balanced rhythmic interchange. There has been much said of one sleeping with the head to the North, or East, or in a particular direction. This is not a fixed law; it varies with each individual. Each person should try the various directions. With some people it would require that they vary direction occasionally.

It is more important to sleep away from metallic objects. Coil springs are especially detrimental to complete rest. Metallic conductors set up vortices that cause a circular motion within the straight lines of force. This is a parallelism to body activity; so

INVISIBLE GEARS

instead of resting, your body is working even while you sleep.

The essence of life is the same in all densities or "dimensions". Life is manifested from the "A" and "B" lines of light force by the infinite "G" light. Life is only given form in the First density by the principle of "the wheel of life".

All vegetation, all substance with form—such as rocks, fluids, and planets—maintains form through various times, stages, or cycles.

Each form of life in the First density contributes substance to every other form of life on all material, or negative levels.

All densities of life contribute to the progression of every form of life in densities beneath them. All forms of substance are alive in repetitive patterns for their particular species. Thus substance, through life, repeats its cycles "from dust to dust".

Life is the carrier of progression in its eternal and endless spiral. Thus the stages are positive ⛨ or negative ⛨ or both ⊕ when they are in balance.

The spiral of life (also called Caduceus) is symbolized by two serpents: ☤ . The negative, receptive, or female ʃ is only given desire by its opposite ⚹, the positive, projective, or male counterpart and vice versa. These symbols are not zigzag in form, they are spiral. They are centered and separated by the "staff of life" ⎸ around which they twine ever upward through the infinite Intelligence.

The First density on Earth, consisting mainly of vegetation, is of both polarities. The dividing line is the surface of the Earth. The positive, projective part of the plant is attracted into the dark negative soil to provide minerals and moisture so the receptive, female portion above the surface may "bloom in her fullness".

This is the reason why a water-witcher's twig, taken from a living plant, can indicate water. It is actually a living instrument. Like magnets when they are cut, the positive end remains in the same direction. Therefore they are held upside down in order to function. As all things beneath the surface of the soil are of negative polarity and since survival is the strongest desire, the twig wants to assume its natural polarity-position and is attracted, positive end butt first, to the "water of life".

For the same reason, when you spend long periods of time in the positive sun, you require more water which is negative, to quench your thirst which is the result of unbalanced light force.

Every cell in the vegetation is life in form, main-

INVISIBLE GEARS

taining a still greater life in form. As an animal eats the First density (stationary Life form) vegetation, it gives to it motion.

The substance confined to the place where the seed dropped can now move around, as it has been assimilated by and raised to the Second density (Life and Motion).

The same progression of substance takes place when you eat the flesh of an animal. Humans being both animal and spirit, are of the Third density (Life, Motion and Consciousness).

You, as part of the eternal pattern of life in form, give to the animal substance the ability to express and recognize the spirit.

Although all forms of life progress within their own densities, much confusion has been started by the theorists who try to tie the densities together. Darwin tried to show the evolution of man from the apes. There is no missing link except breeding.

As our solar system has progressed through space it crossed on August 20, 1953, from the Third density to the Fourth density.

Our planet has emerged from the frequency of the Third density. Everything on this planet must now begin to conform to this higher frequency pattern.

We are on the verge of witnessing a cyclic, planetary housecleaning. All things in this solar system are going to be brought into balance.

The space people of the Adamic race, serving as agents of God, have through the centuries followed a pattern of cycles in bringing their qualified teachers to the people of Earth.

Approximately every 2100 years the spacecraft of the space people have landed one of their Divine Mothers on Earth, to give birth to a "true son of God". As far as the records go, they have all been "virgin mothers".

These cycles are determined by the Adamic people according to cosmic planetary time. A Minor Cycle is approximately 2100 years, or one-twelfth of a Major Cycle.

A Major Cycle is about 26,000 years, or a complete cycle of the Precession of the Equinox. These cycles vary in time either way, plus or minus, according to nutation.

During the last Major Cycle the space people landed twelve teachers. The teacher called Jesus was the twelfth and last of the "sons of God" in the past Major Cycle.

The policy is always to return the last teacher of each Major Cycle to begin the next cycle.

The importance of today is emphasized by the fact that we are not only on the pinnacle of a Minor Cycle, but are also amidst a Major, and Master Cycle at the same time. This brings about a balancing of the planetary forces that the space people call "the Father's housecleaning among His planets". However, in the Bible it is called the time of the great earthquake.

Noah walked with God because he was one of

INVISIBLE GEARS

the space people who came to the Earth in the "arc of Noe".

In the Bible, Noah is confused with Noe. Noah was a man, and Noe was the "arc of Noe".

It was in the "arc of Noe" that the animals were brought to Earth. The space people landed the various animals that could survive in the Second density germination temperature.

Of course there was a flood during the time of the "arc of Noe". The Bible is correct when it said all the water was in the firmament (in the First density). That was why the vegetation was so thick in the First density. The moisture would condense and water the vegetation at night and rise as fog in the daytime.

When the Earth flipped on its poles in the "arc of Noe", the rotational speed changed and the new temperature of the Earth being less, the waters condensed and fell from the atmosphere and flooded the land. The Bible says the waters were fifteen cubits deep (about 27 feet) in Genesis, 7:20.

So the story in the Bible of the ark and its animal cargo, is a badly twisted version of a man and a boat. The size of the Biblical ark is given as 300 cubits long, 50 cubits wide and 30 cubits high, (about 525 feet, by 88 feet wide, by 53 feet high).

Imagine caging a pair of each kind of living thing in an area that large. And don't forget they needed sufficient food carried to feed them for 40 days.

THE COUNCIL OF SEVEN LIGHTS

Then the story gets further off. They confused the accurate, ancient records with another "arc". This was when the Bible story puts Noah's *sons* in the same boat.

The animals were landed in the "arc of Noe", between the First and Second densities. Three hundred and twelve thousand years later Ham, Shem, and Japheth were landed on Earth; between the Second and Third densities, in the "arc of Spae".

Noah's "sons" were not individuals either. The race of Ham were the black people. The race of Shem were white people, and the race of Japheth were the yellow people.

The various tribes that descended from these three original colors of people, that were colonized on Earth by the space people, is listed in Genesis, chapter 10.

Each race is pure in its own color. And the Universal law reads "each seed after its own kind". In all the creations on the Earth, each flower, tree, animal and all of nature follows this Law—except humans who were given the right to choose. Humans were given the intelligence to raise themselves, yet humans are the only creatures that violate this Law.

THE COUNCIL OF SEVEN LIGHTS

O man, though I am One, I am also Many. Though I center the individual light of each of you, you also are the One of Me. I live each sensation; I live every expression; I am the motion of thee, O man. Consider each thing you do, you do to Me. For when you strike one of My parts I feel the blow. And when you cast a thought of love, I absorb the love of you; and I return it too. When idle mind leads thee to tear the reputation of another down, you have only lowered your thought of Me, and in turn have lowered yourself. Realize that I am always with you. Always the silent, unseen, companion to your every action; the recipient of your every thought. I love to express Myself through you in ways that bring Me joy; in paths that reach the hearts in gratitude. Help Me to express the Oneness of each of Us that I may center all My parts in unity of Me and thee in harmony and Love; that none shall know the pain, and sorrow, and heartbreak you did express yourself. I gave thee Light of Life that you might extend My action; that others might feel the Joy of Me that are in darkness bent, who are trouble-blinded and cannot see that I am there. Extend the progress I have brought into being by lifting up another, that I may feel the twofold expression expressed in grateful thanks.

Though I am stillness, My parts all move in Me. My rest is in contrast, or motion could not be. Extremes establish the boundaries beyond which man cannot go. Though I am boundless, man is bound in Being of Me, by individuality.

THE COUNCIL OF SEVEN LIGHTS

Man I have created so I may extend Myself through motion of the parts of Me, so I will not be bound within the stillness of My infinity.

Chapter Three
THE SUNS OF GOD

The Sun is an evolved planet in its progressive state of becoming space. An expanding universe must have something to expand from. The Sun is not becoming smaller by combustion, fission or fusion. It is growing larger by digestion of the matter it encounters in the lines of primary light energy. The Sun gives off only a very small percentage of the energy it is thus acquiring. Matter, or mass, cannot give off but only a small percentage of its actual total potential energy, even in the famed atomic bombs.

The energy given off by any fuel or matter is always less than that substance which went into its making. Why is this?

The answer is — because *Mind* also went into the making of all created things. Mind is neutral. Mind cannot give off energy, it can only direct the flow and action of energy. Universal Mind permeates all things. Each person uses the Mind of God according to his, or her ability to get into It deeper. All things that are, or ever will be, already exist in Universal Mind. None can penetrate into the Universal Mind beyond their own acquired capability. On the other hand, God cannot do more for you than you are capable of doing for yourself by directing the Universal Mind.

THE COUNCIL OF SEVEN LIGHTS

When scientists discovers that the core of the proton in an atom is square, then they will realize that the body in the Sun is also square.

The cubic minerals in their crystallized state are of neutral polarity on a negative surface such as the Earth. They can be brought into polarity however, by exposure to light, pressure, or charging.

The body of the Sun was brought into cubic form by the fact that its axes were parallel to the three lines of light energy. The infinite light (Universal Mind), or the "G" line of light centers one axis. The positive "A" and the negative "B" lines center the other two axes. They are all at 90° angles to each other.

The sunspots are discharges of secondary magnetic (electrostatic) force released into the actisphere and photosphere by the rotating corners of the square core body. These discharges are magnetic exhaust effects common to any body in motion. The sunspots are apparent in the 10° to 30° North and South latitudes on the Sun, to our vision. The sunspots are exhausted when the discharged polarized matter is neutralized in the photosphere or the actisphere. They appear black to Earth telescopes, because they hide the effect of fusion taking place between the positive photosphere and the negative actisphere.

The positive photosphere to the positive Sun body is the equivalent of the negative atmosphere to the negative Earth body — they each carry the same polarity as the body which they surround.

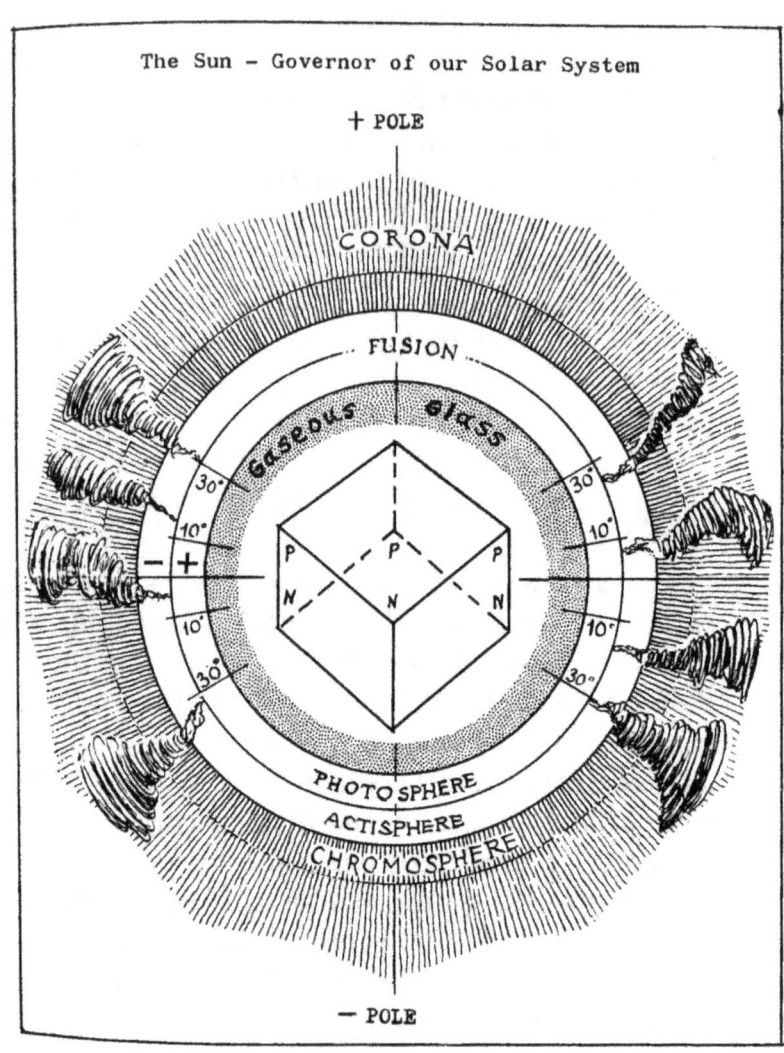

THE COUNCIL OF SEVEN LIGHTS

The fact that the rotational period of the Sun appears to be of different speeds at different latitudes, is due to the spiral effects of primary light energy losing speed in its travel to the poles. The apparent ten day differential in rotation between the equator of the Sun and its poles is only observed in the force field of the actisphere.

Viewed from the point of any of the three axes, a cube will appear square around its perimeter. Many square, positive bodies in space do not rotate, because their axes remain parallel to the lines of primary light.

The bodies that do rotate were placed in motion when their axes were thrown out of parallel with the lines of light, by a bend, or warp in the lines of primary energy. This caused the positive, square body to start rotating by unbalanced polarity opposition within itself.

The polar axis of the Sun is now through two opposite corners of the cubic Sun body. The cube remained motionless in the lines of primary energy, like a compass needle, as long as it was in polarity balance.

Once the body was in motion, the lines of force, trying to reach rest, spiraled to the two points of least motion. This established an equator and opposite poles at two opposite corners.

In this position the positive polarity half, and the negative polarity half of the Sun, each has three corners discharging at approximately 20° each side of the equator. These rotating corners are displacing matter and discharging energy; this is what causes the sunspots.

Cut an artgum eraser, or a piece of soap, into a cube and insert common pins in two opposite corners. Then make a line around the cube midway between the pole points, or pins. Assume one half of the cube will have four corners in it of one polarity. Then if you look at the opposite corners you will find they are all on the other side of the equator line.

You will also see that each half, from the equator line, is a three sided pyramid, or prism. The polarized prismic structure of the rotating Sun generates secondary light in its positive photosphere. The negative actisphere, which we see as a ball of fire, is activated in opposition to the photosphere by the primary lines of light energy.

Space is the cubes of matter that are stable, because their three axes are parallel to the three lines of light. Motion is only manifested by unbalanced matter; whether it be a sun, planet, atom, or person.

Desire for rest is what causes the Intelligence in matter in motion to seek balance and become again part of the infinite Intelligence, which is still. Space is composed of balanced cubes of Intelligence at rest.

The lines of primary light energy parallel the eight edges and two axes of the cubes of space in two directions, and the infinite light parallels the four remaining edges and one axis.

All unbalanced, positive bodies are emitting light.

THE COUNCIL OF SEVEN LIGHTS

All unbalanced, negative bodies are absorbing light. Cubes are unbalanced, positive bodies. Negative bodies are unbalanced spheres. Each can contain, or be a part of the other; as long as one polarity is predominant. The predominant polarity will determine whether the object is spherical or cubical in shape.

Astronomers state that the light from some of the stars is coming from so many hundreds and thousands of light years away, that the star could be burned out and the light would still be visible on the Earth. This is predicated on the idea that the light is still traveling after the emitting body is no longer there. This is erroneous. If the stars were not still emitting light, and were not there, you could not see it.

Telescopes and eyes do not see! They are only a system of lenses through which light passes. The mind sees. You can picture things you have experienced in the mind with your eyes closed.

The same infinite light of Intelligent Mind centers every atom, star, planet, and manifested being. When astronomers look through a telescope, or people observe without one; anything you can see is there. The instant, infinite, light of Universal Mind that centers you and what your mind sees; cannot record, or vision something that is not there.

Negative, physical vision only records to the negative, physical brain the illusion that the Sun is round. All that the limited physical vision is recording is

THE SUNS OF GOD

the effect of the secondary light emissions from the force field in fusion around the Sun.

Physical, negative vision can only see reflected, positive light from another negative body; or negative light reflected from another positive body. The actisphere being of negative polarity, is spherical. Therefore, the negative, physical vision records it as a ball of fire. Were it not for the activation of the Sun's actisphere by the positive and negative lines of primary light energy, you would not see the Sun at all with physical vision.

Though I scatter My seeds of Light throughout My garden of space, I determine which shall grow to be a star and which shall represent My Image.

Though all My seeds are Light of Me, each brings about a pattern individual in destiny of My doing.

Though in the scattering of My seeds some may fall on barren soil, the segregation is within the knowing which shall bear fruit. For in the essence of My Wisdom I breathe not the breath of Life that all My seeds shall grow at once. Rather do I select them that I may express Myself each moment throughout eternal time. And though my seeds are pure in Light and Love of Me, I know all shall not grow to bring about the fruit in perfection. For unto each seed I rendered individuality and right to choose.

O man, O mortal man, My Oneness I bring about in individuality that I may scatter My parts and express Myself. Though all things I have cre-

ated in balanced opposites, I remain the centering separator. Though I have made My gender two, though My polarity is divided, I test My strength on My right and My left. Though man has chosen to further separate My expressions of Love; though man has chosen to divide the roads to Me; though man has brought self-interest into My expression—I still maintain the balance, centering My interchange of powers. If one should sit on My right hand in the Love of Me, I shall balance that Love upon My left hand in equality. I cast out barriers to face the Beings of you, that I may temper all My parts. Though I have given all alike from thought of Me, many cannot reach the door that guides their destiny to paths unfurled in Light. And though they lose their way in darkness—seeking— I retrieve the whole and cast My mold again, never losing any single portion. For I am Soul of thee, O man, and Light and Darkness too. And though my Light of right extends through all eternity, I back the Light with Darkness, that recognition may be yours.

Energy and matter are opposite poles of the same thing. Matter can be converted into energy, but always with mass loss. Energy, in being converted to matter, will always register a gain.

The fact that all celestial bodies are conversions to matter of energy in solution in space, is evidenced by their different densities.

Scientists have assumed that if a rocket could

THE SUNS OF GOD

be propelled outside of the Earth's gravity, it would coast on its momentum indefinitely. This is based on the assumption that space is void. If space were void no system would hold its bodies relative to each other in their orbits.

The "time" field of the Sun establishes a zero field of time relative to the planet's opposition of hemispherical polarities. The opposition of the Earth's polarities relative to the energy charge of its mass is what establishes its position in the solar system.

A small planet can be of greater density than a larger one. Its composition of the elements may be such, however, that its charge relative to its mass may be less.

The "time" field of the Earth is at the magnetic equator. At the Earth's surface it is narrowed down to about the thickness of a razor blade.

Surface land is of greater magnetic potential than the oceans. The Earth's magnetic equator therefore will be inclined to veer toward the major land masses. This wave in the magnetic equator stabilizes as it recedes from the surface.

The angle of divergence is about 5° of arc, making a "V"-shaped cross section as it gains altitude from the surface.

The area composing this "V"-shaped cross section is the Earth's "time" field.

If you could stay in this area a few thousand miles from the Earth's surface, time would cease to exist. Your body polarities would reach balance, and you would become pure Mind and infinite in your scope of everything.

It is the "time" field that separates polarities in their different speeds of apparent rotation.

Relative to the Earth, the positive and negative lines of primary energy are working in opposition. The negative lines of force are causing the Earth to rotate, while the positive lines of force are trying to stop it from rotating. The speed of the Earth's rotation is the result of the differential between the speed of the positive lines of force and the speed of the negative lines of force, relative to the charge of the Earth's mass.

The positive and negative lines of force fill space with matter in solution. Being in solution, it must be termed energy, because it is not condensed by polarity predominance.

The "time" field ends at the outer limit of the Earth's force field. If it were possible to alter the "time" field by changing it relative to the Earth's magnetic equator, we could direct the planet's course out of the solar system, or cause it to assume another orbit elsewhere in the system.

The spacecraft are controlled in their travel by oscillating the "time" field with thought force, causing the positive and negative fields to move the ship's mass relative to the direction of the lines of primary energy.

Earth scientists do not understand negative electrical currents, or fields. As the positive lines of force manifest results through conductors, the negative currents and fields can only be activated through non-conductors. The only true insulation that will separate the opposite polarities of fields is time. The Earth's people only register time because the planet rotates and orbits. They assume that "time goes by". Time is infinite, and all that people on a planet can register is the revolving planet passing through time. The people are in motion on the planet, so they assume that time is in motion. Actually they are moving through time with no visible means of registering the stillness of time. If time ever moves it will cause everything in the universe to collide, and all condensed energy, or matter, would go back into solution in space.

When the scientists try to push a rocket through space by brute force, instead of going with the currents of primary energy carrying matter in solution in space, they will discover that matter in solution (energy) or space is anything but void.

The speed of light, established at 186,000 miles per second, is *not* its speed. It is the speed of the positive "A" lines of force that extend throughout space. The speed of the negative "B" lines of force, at 90° to the positive lines, is 202,000 miles per second. The speed of magnetism is the combined speeds of the positive and negative lines of force, or 388,000 miles per second. The difference between the positive and negative lines of force is 16,000 miles per second.

The space craft use this differential to cycle or phase their power. This accounts for their appearance of skipping. Their ships are caused to attract or repel the lines of force which are at right angles to their direction of travel.

The space craft can move through our dense, lower atmosphere at many thousands of miles per hour, because they bring their own "space" with them. The force field around each ship does not allow our air to enter the field, consequently the ship does not get hot by friction. The ship, inside of its own force field, is protected by the field from debris in space, from air in density, and from sound shock waves. As no sound can penetrate through the field, they travel silently through our skies; except at very slow speeds or when hovering, they transmit a humming, throbbing tone. The field increases its resistance and strength when the speed of the ship increases.

Space is infiltrated with debris. No principle of rocket propelled missiles or ships is practicable outside of our Earth's force field, as rockets do not create a protective field around themselves. Some of the debris, from the size of grains of rice to rocks larger than buildings, are traveling at speeds of hundreds of miles per second.

Our planet operates in a self-generated magnetic field. Meteorites do not burn out in our atmosphere because they encounter oxygen. They disintegrate in the Earth's protective field of force. If the meteorite is negatively charged it disintegrates in the positively charged strata of the force field.

Our space craft—the Earth, operates in a field

vortex of the Sun. The Earth is a combination battery, generator, and motor. Our atmosphere serves as a brush, a field, and a bearing. Our heat comes from our dense, surface atmosphere. The only reason we feel more heat on the side toward the Sun is because the positive Sun causes a "brush effect" in our negative, surface atmosphere. The crust commutator is warmed from resistance and friction; while both rotating the planet as a motor, and generating the force field.

Gravity is not attraction, nor "magnetism". Gravity is "resistance pressure" brought about in all objects, bodies, or substances by the lines of force penetrating them toward the center of the Earth.

The "A" positive (male) projective lines of force are trying to reach discharge, or impregnation in the negative (female) crust.

The "B" negative (female) receptive lines of force are trying to reach fecundation or productive powers from the positive male core.

The two lines of force "A" and "B" are working together, in opposition, to supply power for the continuous functions on and in the sphere and atmosphere, while the Father centers the balanced control through the "G" lines of light.

Since the negative lines of force move faster than the positive lines, a negative body will always rotate counterclockwise from one viewpoint, and a positively charged body will rotate clockwise from the same viewpoint.

The measurable speed of positive or negative lines

of light energy will vary with the orbit of any planet. Measurements of light energy of positive polarity will conform to the orbit diameter of any given planet. Measurements of negative polarity light energy will exceed the orbit diameter. Negative light energy cannot be accurately measured from the surface of a negatively charged planet, such as the Earth.

When the atmosphere of negative nature, such as the Earth's, is balanced by positive charges from fusion particles, it will cause moisture in the atmosphere to pile up at one magnetic pole and recede from the opposite polarity pole. It will cause a change in the planet's rotation speed; and due to germination temperature change, the eventual extinction of life forms that conform to that germination temperature. An excess of positively charged particles in the negative atmosphere will cause a planet to seek balance on new poles.

Positive and negative lines of light force are always in an unbalanced state due to their different speeds of travel. When they are interrupted by a body or planet, they bring about motion because of their differential, or the desire to reach rest.

If the Earth's poles were vertical instead of inclined, the Earth's orbit would be round instead of elliptical. If there were as much land south of the Equator as there is north of it, the Earth's axis would not be inclined.

Magnetism is not the causal force, but is the result or exhaust effect of light forces of positive and negative polarity in action. A magnet is not *charged* with magnetism. It is only serving as a polarity conductor of the lines of light energy passing through it. Both poles will *attract* a non-polarized conductor. Either pole will attract its opposite polarity or repel a like polarity.

Influences of a negative nature lead the minds of humans to try to bring about positive effects. When these positive effects exceed the balance of natural negative charges on a negative planet, then the planet will rebalance itself to conform to the light lines of force.

Man is mostly space, filled with substance in form. The body does not derive energy from the food assimilated by it. The food is only transformed to become a conductor for light energy passing through the body.

Power is only manifested through motion. Controlled power is that which is given direction. The discovery of the wheel gave mankind the means to an endless track of motion.

Universal power throughout infinite space is demonstrated in the guided motion of all planets, moons, suns, galaxies, and nebulae. None of these are haphazardly flying through space uncontrolled. Their course, orbit, rotation, and separation are maintained by precision interchange of relative power. All bodies in space are motored by primary light energy. Solar emanations and atomic energy are secondary powers or effects of the primary light energy in motion.

The cross, in one shape or another, has always

been the symbol of spiritual power. Scientifically, spiritual power is unseen power. Spiritual power can only be understood when it is manifest in the seen effect. This seen effect may be either in the range of the physical vision or outside of the physical limits.

Primary light energy functions in many unlimited conditions and frequencies above and below the limits of physical vision. Everything in space that rotates, orbits, or manifests motion as to direction, is powered by primary light energy. Wherever a body interrupts the lines of primary light, motion is effected. This is an immutable law.

Within the human body is a universe in miniature. The axis of every crystal, atom, planet, or person is centered in unseen light of unlimited extent. The manifested boundaries or surface of any of these are insulated from all others of like polarity. The eternal existence of all of these is encompassed within the center of the axis.

The cross is the symbol of power of the opposite polarities. By interrupting the primary lines of positive and negative light energy, a differential is established. By phasing this differential, controlled power is established in motion. This is the long hidden secret of the Maltese cross. "Mal" means negative tongues of flame, or static electricity; "tese" means interchange, two-in-one or differential between. When the differential between the positive and negative forces of light energy are controlled by phasing they result in unlimited power through mo-

THE SUNS OF GOD

tion. If the motion exceeds the differential phase, disintegration will result.

Electricity is a by-product of magnetism. Gravity is the resistance pressure set up by the opposition of differential between the causal light energy and the effect-magnetism.

THE COUNCIL OF SEVEN LIGHTS

Though I have set the patterns of My doing all about you, yet you see them not. I scatter seeds of Light, I cast the shadows man calls day, and shadows of the shadows man calls night, in repetition. I have paved the way for man to see. Has not My pattern stood the test to build another bird a nest again, where others were before? Cannot you see, O man of Me—do as I say, do as I do. Do as I cause the way to be, within your understanding of the Me in thee. Look to the pattern all around; the fragrance of the essence of My Love in flowers you have found; and in the cool, beneath the tree, there I am to comfort you—and yet you question parts of Me. Throughout My Being, I made thee man to carry on; to take the stand in My defense; to build the wall, to scale the fence of destiny. Not to follow whims of chance along the side; not to fall beneath the wheels of hate and fear, that others may ride in comfort. Only look, feel the essence of My Being. Absorb Me in the breeze. Reach Me in the sun. My heart is warm, you are the one. Never have I set a pattern to lead you all astray. Any fear you feel, O man, you make along the way to Me and your arrival is delayed. Your stage is set, the curtain must come down, but only to go up again. My pattern is eternity. Repetition is the grade that leads to Me, O man.

From the harvest of My golden grain I separate the chaff. I break the bonds of freedom, lest man shall undo My works. I bring about a change in cycles so My balance shall not be disturbed.

THE COUNCIL OF SEVEN LIGHTS

For when My Laws are superseded, then must I strike from out the night and scourge contamination from My Being.

For I am Love, and I am freedom unto all My parts, but no part shall bind Me to destruction.

So as in times gone past; I wreak My wrath, I cleanse My house, I upset My creations—for none shall be above Me!

Chapter Four

TRINITY OF INFINITY

Time is only understood by each conscious, intelligent unit from its established point of location in motion.

Time cannot be measured, only the repetition of motions manifested as beginnings and endings can be measured.

Each point of beginning and ending is only relative to the understanding of the individual establishing his point of view.

The point of begin and end is established by one individual, so as to bring another individual to the same point of understanding.

Life, time and Be-ing are understandable to Intelligence alone. These three are non-existent only when Intelligence has been excluded by ignorance in the individual.

Life, time and Be-ing can only exist in space, which is also infinite.

Space is solution, composed of Life, time, Be-ing, and Intelligence. None of these can be measured in the Absolute. They can only enter measurable dimension when individuals establish points from which to measure.

Length, height, and width; these are only three measurements by which individuals can understand

TRINITY OF INFINITY

points from which relative measurements are started and ended.

An inch, a foot, or a yard, are not understood by people who use some other devised means of measurement. A relative difference between the measurements must be charted in order to understand the difference between their system and ours.

Measurements can only be achieved in and by motions. No day or night could be measured without the motion of the Earth revolving. No seasons or years would exist if the Earth didn't orbit around the Sun.

The life span of people on the Earth is only arrived at by the measurement of people's time on Earth relative to past measurements. Belief (the illusion of reality) makes people accept the established record of the life spans of other people who have lived before them, as a measure by which they should live and then die.

The establishment of these points of beginning and end of life are only manifest in matter which has little or no Intelligence.

Matter cannot manifest motion without energy. Energy is the motion of thought manifested through matter. Intelligence which has no motion can only manifest through thought, which causes motion to be manifest in matter by thought force.

In symbology the Creator is expressed by $\bigodot$.

This signifies the circumference encompassing everything. The circle is an endless line signifying infinity with no beginning and no end.

Life is an essence of the infinite solution we call space. You are living in an endless ocean of life, as are the atoms, planets, and suns. You could not manifest life, if life were not where you are. Since life manifests everywhere in infinity, you cannot end life, or begin life. You can only establish a point in the endless circle ⊙ where you began the cycle of manifesting matter in life.

Motion can be symbolized in the endless circle by the sign of an arrow ⊙ . An arrow has always signified "the way to go". All matter manifesting life in balanced motion moves in an arc. All matter manifesting life in unbalance, or un-natural principles, is symbolized by an angle ⊙ .

The largest portion of you is space, whether it be the space in atoms, cells, or tissue composing the matter of your physical body; or the space your limited body as a unit occupies.

Your intelligence is established by the limits of your individual concepts. Everyone uses the One Mind. Your limit is only a measurement of your ability to penetrate and absorb to the full your capacity of the infinite Intelligence.

Time is variable in your concept of it. One day seems longer, or shorter, than another day.

TRINITY OF INFINITY

You are an assembly of other forms of individual manifested life. You are a form enclosing various compositions of atomic, molecular, crystalline, and cellular structure. In turn you are a small individual part of a living planet, solar system, and galaxy.

Change is the result of motion. Time is measurable only in cycles of repetition.

Every thought sets up motion. Every motion causes an effect. Your manifestation of matter in motion is the reflection of your true concept, and understanding, of Infinity.

Things in motion change, and things that change are not eternal in any one pattern of form.

"T" is the symbol of time.
"S" is the symbol of space.
"B" is the symbol of Being.

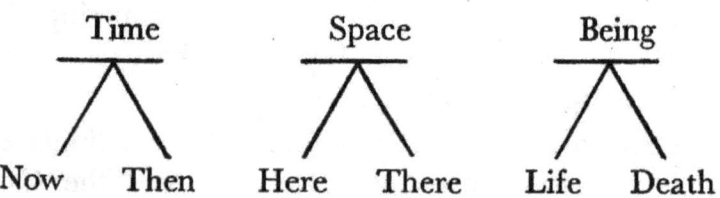 is the Caduceus, or the triune of "T", "B", and "S". Division of the eternal things is what created opposites.

Time	Space	Being
/\	/\	/\
Now Then	Here There	Life Death

Cycles are repetitions of the divisions. All divisions of opposites reach a fulcrum pinnacle of stillness, at times. Everything in the universe comes under one, or the other, of the three aspects of infinity.

Each of the opposites, such as here and there,

cycles an interchange within itself like a swinging pendulum.

"Here" becomes "there" as soon as you cross the street, and "there" becomes "here". As you register your own changes in time, "tomorrow" becomes "today" as the Earth revolves on its axis, and "today" was "tomorrow" yesterday.

Life and death also interchange, so that Being may manifest through the action.

Time cannot be a dimension, because everything in motion in time will never repeat itself again exactly as it was before.

If you could be *not*, then you could not be *now*, because now was then before you arrived here from there. You *are* all the time, even when your body sleeps. The real You never sleeps, although it rests at the peak of the fulcrum in the interchange between the opposites of life and death.

Flesh is only matter you assimilate as a requirement of this dense Earthly condition. Flesh moves only because your real body moves it. Your matter body of flesh is not going to walk, or talk, after you get out of it. *Death* can only manifest in matter. This is the interchange that permits matter to return to what it was before you assimilated it into form.

That portion of space which is *You*, will always *Be* in *time* somewhere. Expressing *life here now* is really *death there then*, when you observe from the opposite side of things.

TRINITY OF INFINITY

The trinity of time, space, and Being are the deity called God.

Time, like thought, is infinite. Time does not "go by". Everything that moves in the universe goes *through* time.

Man measures time with clocks and calendars. If there were no measuring methods made by man, then there would be no yesteryears or tomorrows. Age would not exist, today would be all there is.

Individual beings are all part of each other in the universal sense, making up Infinite Being. God is not an individual, but is all of us. God being infinite and boundless, He is not something or someone man finds on the other side of the door called death. If this were true, He would not be infinite.

Time is a medium through which the beings of God's creation manifest God's Presence. No one can live in the past or the future who is not present now in God.

Mind through thought is not limited to the present, for thought is also infinite. The Creative Mind of today is the same infinite Mind that created the universe. Mind is God manifested in Be-ing. Your part of God is manifested when you use God's infinite Mind to create through thought. Thought is the creative force that gives Life to Be-ing.

Space is not void. Space is the essence of Intelligent Mind. Man is a space filled with creative matter, manifesting the thought essence of form. And so are all things with life.

Man is in God's Image only when the thought of

infinite Mind is brought into being by individual thought—to manifest other creative forms in time.

Objects, structures, and things cannot manifest creative thought; as they do not move through infinite time as individual parts of space, or the essence of Intelligence.

To be, man must manifest motion in the medium of time, which stands still. Anyone who does not "have time" to manifest God's doing, has discarded thought and life. The matter manifesting their form will soon become inert. Death is not "a doorway to God in heaven". Heaven is a doorway to God on Earth.

THE COUNCIL OF SEVEN LIGHTS

Mortals bound in density who would be the cause, who would bide my time, the tree of thee in Me stops not its growth. Though My parts would add to My divisions, My faceless cosmic clock records no time. For man is not a cause, but rather a result of Me, for I alone am cause of things to be. And though thou mortal man would wind My clock of destiny, and set the powder keg of destruction at My feet, how can he know the woe? For I alone am cause and man is the result of Me, bound to destiny. And in destruction-bent reverses course and all the Light spent in his Being is hidden by the curtain of ignorance drawn before Me. Though I alone am cause, My wrath is not aroused. I tear the shroud. I bring man back through birth within the Light, and test My right expressed in progression of My parts. I write the drama, man plays the fool, then I applaud and make the tool sharper to My cause through experienced results. Man cannot set My clock, for I alone can read the time of My eternity. And so it is—I set the stage, I play the parts, I cause the curtain to come down while man sits in the audience of My universe applauding, not knowing why.

Though I have scattered My creations throughout the endless space of Me, I use My tools to manifest My doings.

To do My works no task is small. I choose My tools, I trust them all until they fail Me. Then I put another to the test.

My tools are not the tools of man, that rust and

break and fall away. My tools are living instruments that work with love throughout the day and night.

To each I gave the choice to be an instrument of Me.

Chapter Five
UNSEEN SCALES

The accompanying drawing is to explain the one universal principle of Life. This principle is standard on any planet in space, and in all life forms, whether insect, animal, bird, human, Man or spirit.

In the drawing you are looking at the cut ends of the negative "B" lines of light energy—of course greatly enlarged. They are traveling away from you and rotating in a counter-clockwise direction. These are the female, receptive, negative polarity lines of light energy.

At right angles, or 90° to the "B" lines of light energy are the positive "A" lines, traveling from left to right and rotating in a clockwise direction.

These two lines of light energy can only unite in birth or death. Birth by induction, and death by shortcircuiting.

God controls physical birth and death by allowing the rebirth of individuals through the living instruments of His choosing. Only when He removes His insulating qualities can a seed be born into another repetition of life progression.

Only when you have lived His purpose for you, in each life grade, does He graduate you into the next grade.

If your actions prove to Him that through violation of His infinite laws you will not pass this grade,

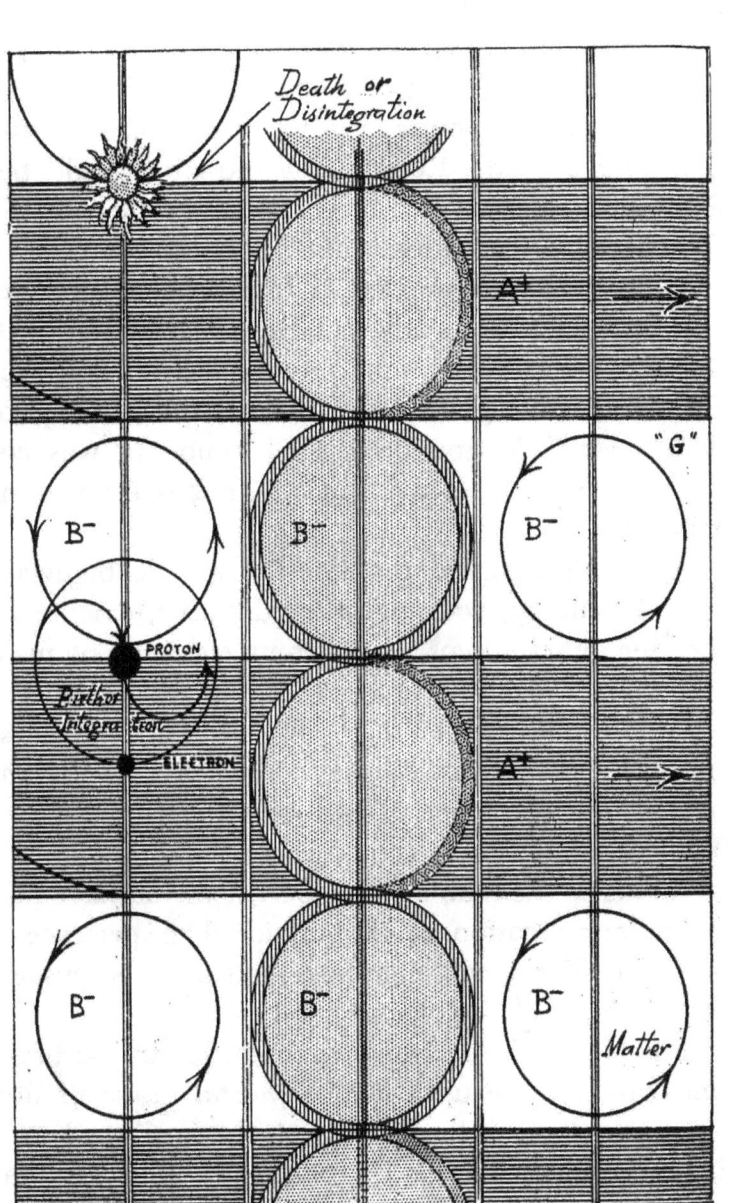

UNSEEN SCALES

then you die physically and your eternal, atomic cluster of consciousness is brought back through rebirth into the same grade in order to pass on to the next higher grade. Rebirth into the same grade, because of failure to pass it, is the only time that the so-called "reincarnation" takes place.

When you were created as Man in God's Image, you were made an atom of matter, charged with opposite polarities in your proton-electron individuality. You were given individual motion. The space within your electron orbit shell boundary was endowed by the Creative Spirit with His unseen Intelligence.

As you progressed through the mobile highways of light energy, you encountered the experience of meeting other atoms of different elements of matter. With each new experience you added another atom to your consciousness. Soon the consciousness began to increase in size, composed of many atoms of different experiences and of different elements. Your consciousness is composed of the same number of atoms as the number of experiences you have had since your creation as an individual. Experience is recorded in the consciousness. And in consciousness is the eternal record of your knowing.

Education and learning are recorded in the brain and can only be used in this *mortal* grade of life. When the brain is buried with the body all the learning and intellectual education ends, unless it has been applied through experience.

To reach the true Intelligence of your many experiences and permanent knowledge requires going within; through meditation you can become aware of your consciousness and unseen Intelligence you accumulated in the past.

The largest portion of your original atom creation was the space within the shell boundary. This space is, was, and will always be the unseen portion of your part of the Supreme Intelligence.

As you travel through the maze of life lines you often encounter resistance, set up by those who think they are going in the right direction and that you should conform to their direction of travel. But each was given the individual right to choose his direction. Scientifically the correct course is at 45° to the lines of light, and in a progressive spiral into finer frequencies of light. This maintains the balance between the positive and negative lines of light energy.

Every body that interrupts the lines of force will establish a "field" around itself.

Stationary bodies such as trees, rocks, or mountains, establish "fields" the same as atoms, planets, or suns. On a surface of negative polarity the *height* of every species is established by the "field" around it; therefore vegetation and trees grow to a common species average.

The "field" set up in a tree is such that the lines of force passing through the tree establish a vortex in its body. This vortex starts at the surface of the ground. Sap does not only go up a tree but it goes around in a spiral, as it goes up.

UNSEEN SCALES

The *shape* of each plant, or stationary form of life, is established by the boundaries of its vortex or its field, or its aura. Everything everywhere is encompassed in such an auric field.

In life that moves, such as animals, the soul force in the body establishes form from the central, intelligent, master cell. This frequency of the animals is much lower than the human form, of course.

The animal body of humans is the manifested filler, composed of inert matter, that is required in the frequency upon the Earth's surface. The soul force is distributed through the inert matter by the blood stream. The Man body of Reality establishes the "field".

In climbing a hill you have to push the vortex upward. It is much easier for some people to so climb than others. This is because their polarity balance is nearer to neutrality. If the physical, negative vortex, surrounded by the aura, reaches a balance between what we term "spirit" and the "physical", that person can climb a hill without effort because it is not required that he push the inert matter upward in defiance of the laws of gravity.

The human vortices also start and end at the surface of the ground. In man, balance is achieved above the Earth's surface. The negative vortex has its apex downward, at the feet. The positive vortex of the Real body has its apex upward, above the head.

When the balance between the physical reflection and the real body, or the consciousness of your Being, reaches a state of equilibrium, these vortices will be of the same length, the same diameter, and the same speed of rotation. You can levitate yourself with the forces established at a zero point between these two opposing polarities.

Through these vortices, and with them you can establish a "field" of protection around you. Not necessarily by willful direction but by the actions you manifest. If your thought is good your actions are of a giving nature; if you are concerned with the welfare of others you automatically establish a "field" of protection around you because the Universal Mind compensates directly, and equally, for every thought and action.

The zero balance between the physical vortex and the vortex of the Real, conscious, everlasting You, is difficult to hold. You may be unbalanced slightly in one direction or the other; in one belief or the other; in the manifested actions you perform.

The purpose in your being on the surface of the planet is to bring about a balance, first, in your own control, and next, a balance between each of you; an understanding, a compassion, a love that is not expressed in words. This balance cannot be maintained mechanically, for you don't know which vortex to increase, or decrease. But by following the basic principle of the *Golden Rule,* by doing all things in moderation, you will arrive at a point of equilibrium where you will be able to know which side of zero you must bring up, or down. When you reach a state of zero polarity between your individual vortices, you are at One with the infinite Mind. You can know anything, you can see anything, and you can be anything of your own choice, so long as you maintain that balance.

If you associate closely with people, these vortices can leak; thereby causing you to acquire disease or character conditions of ones you associate with. This is also responsible for what we call love. Not the real love, but the physical attraction of one for another, oftentimes of one sex for the same sex. If one has a predominantly negative, physical vortex and another has a predominantly spiritual vortex, these two vortices are attracted to each other. This is not the condition of love. It is a condition of mutual attraction by two people, who may seem to be entirely opposite in every other respect.

Someone at a distance from you cannot affect you, but in close association you will assimilate characteristics of another person. These are natural things, because nature wants to balance everything.

The spiritual person is attracted to the predominant materialist, and vice-versa.

The leakage of vortices is something you should watch for. You can assimilate character, understanding, and love by association with people who demonstrate these characteristics. Therefore you should try to associate with these types of people.

The vortex of the human physical body will also cause people to be repelled. Oftentimes you will meet one whom you immediately dislike intensely. This is not a condition of knowing the other person;

it is a natural condition of polarities repelling each other.

These things are beyond the scale of records, as far as individuals go. It is not possible to compute, and understand, the vortices of all individuals.

Individually however; you can try to understand your own, and the effects of the vortices of other people upon you.

But remember, one can be close to you and discharge your vortex by an opposite charge, thereby causing you to feel physically tired and drained of life.

Study your friends at a safe distance (about six feet) before you associate closer, or you may discover what you term an enemy in the friendship you thought was yours.

THE COUNCIL OF SEVEN LIGHTS

O man, My Light is not for the victor, nor for the one who falls in defeat; My Light is to the one who gains understanding of My ways. My arms are not extended either to the right or the left, but are centered to balance the living individual parts of My Being. Though forces may oppose your every move, My strength lies in the power to meet the opposition. Though evil may tempt you, My Light is brightest when the evil is overcome. For evil is not of My creation, O man. Evil is brought about by those who falter on the way to Me. Never, never in all My eternity shall man control the paths to Me. The paths are My ways, and man can only travel on My paths. In all My doings I have brought about a pattern of progression. None can turn about My works, none can interrupt My way. Those who follow in the darkness only trip themselves. Stand within the Light of Me; for I am Light of thee, O man; and I can only shine when you have made the way in progress of My doing. Lean not upon another, only accept thy brother as one to help one to assist along the way, that unity in numbers may bring about progress in My infinite Light. Fear not, fear not! There is no fear within My Being of you. Fear is only added by the things you do that are not within the pattern of My ways. Reach within, I am there. None can scare you when you find the Me in thee. Stand, stand upright. Death is only that which adds to those who have performed the grade. Fear no evil, stand within My Light. Feel My living Light within you. Know that I am there throughout eternity.

CHAPTER SIX

THE ANGELS OF SPACE

"And the angel that talked with me came again, and waked me, as a man that is wakened out of his sleep." (Zechariah 4:1).

This paragraph fits almost exactly the experience that I had on August 24th of 1953.

Angels were always considered by me to be some vaporous type of afterlife that just floated about here and there. My entire concept of things changed with the physically manifested appearance of one of these angels to me.

From the position of the full Moon, I judged it to be around 2 A.M. Here on the desert it is nearly as bright in full moonlight as it is in daylight. I awakened, not knowing why, but sensing that something had happened that had disturbed me. We sleep outside about six months out of the year, so you can see that our bedroom was readily accessable.

As I looked up from the bed I saw a man standing about six feet away from the foot of the bed. This was not uncommon, as we operate a public airport and have been awakened many times by our dogs barking at people coming in during the night. However, at this time not a sound was heard from the dogs. This I recalled later and it was certainly unusual.

I asked the man what he wanted, thinking his

car might have given him trouble and he had walked into our remote airfield as many others have done before. At the same time I sat up in bed. Beyond the man, about a hundred yards away, hovered a glittering, glowing spaceship, seemingly about eight feet off the ground.

I knew then that he was not having car trouble. The man said, "My name is Solgonda. I would be pleased to show you our craft."

My left hand and arm were still under the covers. I pinched my wife in the side to awaken her. Solgonda smiled, like he knew what I was doing. I pinched her again. She normally awakens very easily. I didn't want her to miss what was taking place. Solgonda smiled again. Still no response from my wife, so I pinched her hard. Solgonda nearly laughed aloud. My wife didn't wake up and somehow I realized Solgonda had her under some kind of control.

I hopped out of bed clad only in under-shorts. Solgonda preceeded me for a few yards and then I caught up with him and walked beside him. Not a word was said as we walked to the ship. In fact, I never said another word to him.

From the time I got out of bed, until I returned to it, every time I thought of something to say he was answering me before I could speak the first word of any sentence. This proved to me their perfect ability to communicate by thought transference.

As we approached the craft I began to get butterflies in my stomach from about fifty feet away. Coming nearer, my hair seemed to want to stand up on end. This feeling disappeared instantly upon entering the ship.

The craft was about 36 feet in diameter and about 19 feet high. It looked like the same type that George Adamski photographed in his close-ups.

The interior was about 18 feet in diameter and about 10 feet high. The walls were of some opalescent material like our imitation mother of pearl. There was a shelf around the inside below the portholes, about elbow height from the floor when one was standing. A column extended from the ceiling to the floor in the center of the ship.

Three other men were on the craft when we went in. They were all of the same approximate height of Solgonda, who was about 5 feet 7 inches tall. These three men smiled but never spoke, and I didn't learn their names.

Solgonda demonstrated their retractable seats, which formed a lounge when extended out of the walls. He showed me several celestial navigation instruments, and then we went below the main deck through a manhole into the power generating room.

Below the deck it was necessary to crouch down on a circular catwalk. There the power mechanism was exposed to view, and I understood the principle of operation, which Solgonda apparently picked up by "telethought".

We left the ship after what I judged to be 20

minutes. Solgonda walked back to bed with me, where my wife was peacefully sleeping. When I climbed back in bed I wondered if the strange feeling I had had in my stomach was going to affect me in any way. Before I could put the thought into words Solgonda said, "No, you'll be all right", and instantly disappeared.

About a minute later the ship slipped slowly into the sky and was out of sight in less than a minute.

Later we checked the hovering spot with a magnetic compass. The vortex set up by the field from the ship would swing the needle 10° easterly in walking into the vortex center, and 5° westerly in passing out of the center on the opposite side.

People who went there a week later to eat their lunch became nauseated and couldn't eat.

I know now that angels are *people* that come out of space. They not only colonize planets and communicate by thought, but they spend their time helping other people to understand Life. Right now they are around and on our planet to help humanity out of the mess we have gotten ourselves into.

People are people *everywhere* in the Creator's universe. The only difference is that most of them have followed the universal laws and thereby progressed, while we on Earth have not.

You had a body before you came here on Earth and you'll have another one when you leave. But maybe then you'll be called an angel.

Genesis tells of God making Man, but it doesn't

THE COUNCIL OF SEVEN LIGHTS

say anything about Him making angels. This further proved to me that angels are the race of *Man*.

The first mention of an angel in the Bible comes in Genesis 16:7. In this verse the angel is referred to as "an angel of the Lord".

The sages of Biblical times knew the mysteries and actions of the esoteric laws. Thus it was known to them that everything that was motivated by natural forces traveled in an arc, or curved path. Anything that moved in any other path of motion was unnatural and was symbolically termed an "angle". People living in Abram's time therefore referred to anything that was of an unnatural motion from their point of view on the Earth's surface, as an "angle".

These people didn't know anything about weather baloons, modern airplanes, and high flying jets. The only things they knew of that flew in the sky were winged birds.

When they observed a spacecraft, or men come out of the sky, they naturally pictured them with wings, like the birds.

Since the appearance of men or ships in the sky was not a naturally happening occurrence, they symbolized the sky visitors as "angles".

The way these people recorded any happening was to have one of their scribes write it down. Like a newspaper reporter of today who wasn't present at the actual scene, the scribe had to write it as it was described to him by eyewitnesses.

THE ANGELS OF SPACE

Whenever the people wanted a copy of any written record, they found a scribe to copy it for them. The scribes of those days got things twisted as badly as the reporters and newspapers of today do.

Due to error in interpreting the symbol, the scribes in copying the accounts of the "angles" coming out of the skies wrote "angel", instead of "angle". All copies made from an erroneous one usually repeated the same mistake. So Angles became Angels.

In a number of the experiences describing contacts with the people in the spacecraft, the Earth people making the contacts stated that the space people "disappeared" before their eyes.

As this also occurred to me during my contact I can understand their amazement. The uninformed would say they "dematerialized". The technically-minded people would say "they went into the fourth dimension". The psychiatrist would say that the people suffered from hallucinations. *None of these are true.*

The reason our space friends can "disappear" is because our physical vision depends on light reflection off of things in order to see. The wave length of visible light extends from approximately 4000 Angstroms (extreme violet) to 7700 Angstroms (extreme red). Compared with the known radiation spectrum as a whole, the range of physical vision is *extremely* limited. This is comparable to looking at the landscape through a crack between two boards, and saying the landscape outside the range of visibility doesn't exist, has dematerialized, or is a hallucination.

Our space friends know LIGHT inside out and backwards. In order to eliminate the need for weapons which would injure others, they have developed what they call the "perfect defense".

This is a small object about two by two inches square and about one half inch thick. It has rounded corners and is generally carried on a cord around the neck and suspended under the blouse.

Their ability to read thoughts allows them to be aware of any danger or threat, and all they have to do is tap this device with either hand; and then appear to disappear.

The object is actually a "crystal battery" that stores "piezo" electricity that is generated by cutting magnetic lines of force, or the same as static electricity.

The nearest thing to this electricity stored by the "crystal battery" that we know of, we refer to as the "spirit body", or aura.

The electrical, spirit body of people varies with their environment, and the chemical make-up of their physical body. This is why you feel good when you are with some people, and feel drained, or exhausted, after association with others. Some people have stronger spirit bodies than others.

When the scoutship landed here in August of 1953, I observed this object. Solgonda was turning it by the corners between his hands. Suddenly he opened

THE ANGELS OF SPACE

two opposite ends of it and pointed it at the granite rocks of the mountain. I saw a pencil-lead-size stream of light between the object and the mountain. I thought he was shooting something near the mountain. Later he explained that he was charging the device. He said they charge various other pieces of their equipment over granite mountains. This is due to the piezo-electric effect set up by quartz in its granite matrix.

When they discharge the "crystal battery" by pressing on either side of it, it releases the charge into their electric body, or aura, and causes light to bend around them; therefore appearing to disappear to the limited physical vision of anyone who is watching them.

They do not dematerialize or go into any other dimension. They are just as solid and physical as always, but they are outside of the limits of physical vision.

This same device was used by the man Jesus when he "disappeared" out of crowds of people, and again when he "re-appeared" unto the people after three days.

In St. Luke 24:13-21, it tells how two of the people walked down the road talking with him.

Verse 31 says, "And their eyes were opened, and they knew him; and *he vanished out of their sight*".

Some teachings would have you believe that this was a vision the people had. Jesus discounted this himself in St. Luke 24:36-39 when he said, "handle

THE COUNCIL OF SEVEN LIGHTS

me, and see; for a spirit hath not flesh and bones, as ye see me have".

Two women shall be grinding together; *the one shall be taken,* and the other left. Two men shall be in the field; the *one shall be taken,* and the other one left. (St. Luke 17:35, 36).

Either you have faith in the prophecy of the Bible, or you must reject the whole book. The Bible is an accurate history of events that repeat themselves in cyclic repetition.

The above paragraphs say a division of humankind will be made. *One shall be taken* and one shall be left. Who is to make the decision? Who will do this judging of humanity to see who will be taken and who will be left?

Every day that passes, you, individually, are establishing your right to be taken *by the way you live.* You are manifesting your choice by your actions and thinking.

Each person adds increase to their vibratory body aura by conforming to the laws of the universe. Your aura, or the frequency of the body force field, will determine whether you are taken or left.

A definite vibration will be established in the force field surrounding each spacecraft that will pick up people. If your body aura or force field conforms with, or exceeds, the established level of the spacecraft force field, then you can enter the ships.

Remember, *you* are *now* qualifying or disqualifying *yourself* to be taken aboard. None can qualify another. Jesus can't "save" you.

Some narrow-minded sects of religious fanatics have established that only 144,000 people will be saved. Of course *they* are part of the chosen few. Those who will be *taken,* and those who will be *saved,* are two separate conditions.

The next thing one asks is, "Where will the people who are picked up be taken?" This is answered in St. Luke 17:37. "And they answered and said unto him, Where, Lord? And he said unto them, Wheresoever the *body* is, thither will the *eagles* be gathered together."

Naturally the eagles gather together in the sky. This was said in a parable at that time, because the people in the Biblical days didn't know what it was to fly in the skies. It was not meant for the people of those days. It was said for the people of *our time.*

The space people (angels) explained that the people who have been taken aboard their craft in these times, were not taken aboard because they were better than anyone else. They explained that these people were taken aboard for *their own test purposes;* to see how different types of people would react. Each one who has been so honored was readily accessable in a remote place. They were of cooperative minds, and each represented a different type of the Earth's people.

This mass pickup of people will take place prior to the planet's rebalancing on new poles. This cataclysm will wipe out the destructive mammon lover who will *be left on the surface.*

After the Earth has re-stabilized on its new poles and the continents and oceans have changed, the people who have been taken up in the air will be landed back on the surface.

"Watch ye therefore, and pray always, that y may be accounted worthy to escape all these thing that shall come to pass, and to stand before the *Son of man.*" (St. Luke 21:36).

THE COUNCIL OF SEVEN LIGHTS

O man, in the rings established within the Light of Me, orbiting My systems—I am potency that moves a nebula, that causes suns to shine. Though some upon this portion of Myself have devious ways to violate My infinite Wisdom, it is not I who judge nor pay the price. As in My cycles, as in My phases, as in My eons, I have established precision in the order of My parts. And though a voice comes through to you unrecognized by mortals, realize, in the voice, I am the potent substance-force of Life, pulsing through your Being, unto eternity. I separate the white from black and color boundaries do I set, for all My creations are of Me, from lowest animal to tree, and all that is. I am the unseen force that manifests in everything you do. Impotent substance-clay of Me cannot interfere, except to bring about conditions that reflect upon the garment that you wear.

O man, never shall you find an end to Me. There is no place I cannot be and am.

You make your hell by deeds you do in violation of My ways. One who says "hell is a place in My infinity", is violating Me.

Reaction is the only hell, rebounding from a spell when you excluded Me, O man!

Some preach there is a hell for others, never for themselves. Watch out for these—their ego is leading them astray.

Through space and time and place, remember I am there and here with you.

THE COUNCIL OF SEVEN LIGHTS

I have no hell for man of Me. Man who believes there is a hell, is reviving imagery of experiences he has had along the road to Me.

CHAPTER SEVEN

PRODIGAL MOTHER

The levels or strata of substance around the crust of the Earth are separated by insulations of the One Still Light. These layers of insulation are the activating Intelligence of the Creator in relation to our planet. Intelligence infiltrates all of the matter in the substance strata. Each alternate matter strata is of opposite polarity and rotates opposite to the matter strata on each side of it.

The Earth is a battery; the strata are the plates. God separates and centers all things through the "G" lines of Still Light. He activates all things through the "A" positive, and "B" negative lines of force.

The center of our planet consists of a sun. This sun, as the core, rotates in the opposite direction to the moving crust.

Between the fiery center of the positively charged core and the negative crust is an insulating, non-conductive strata of fluid glass (obsidian), six hundred miles in thickness.

All ruptures of the crust are caused by *atmospheric* conditions. There are several well-defined areas on the surface of the Earth where vortices of magnetic energy are located. In due time these vortices will bring about the rupture of the crust— termed volcanic action. The earthquake faults were brought about by interruptions of the force field around the Earth.

Planets without moisture in their atmosphere do not rotate. As the "A" and "B" lines of force enter the atmosphere and the crust of the planet, parallel to the Equator and at 90° from each other and the axis, they spiral to each pole and arrive there before the planet has made one quarter of a turn. Emitting from the poles, they encounter resistance in the form of uninterrupted "A" and "B" lines of force, bringing about the phenomena termed aurora.

Every planet in the universe moves in curved lines of travel. This is not because they were thrown off by a sun, or central body. If they were, they would not orbit. Anything thrown off of a rotating object will travel in a straight line outward, though on the Earth it may fall because of gravity. The reason planets or electrons orbit around a central body is because they are powered by light energy.

Space outside of the Earth's atmosphere is blacker than the blackest ink. Our Sun looks like any other bright star, not like a ball of fire. Only the brightest stars can be seen.

Pictured in the drawing is what has often been termed "the four dark corners". The Positive Quarter, or Spring Season of the Earth's orbit, is only predominantly positive relative to the Earth's passing through it. At all other times when light energy is not interrupted by a body or planet, the negative or female lines of force predominate. The old axiom "women first" is applicable throughout the universe.

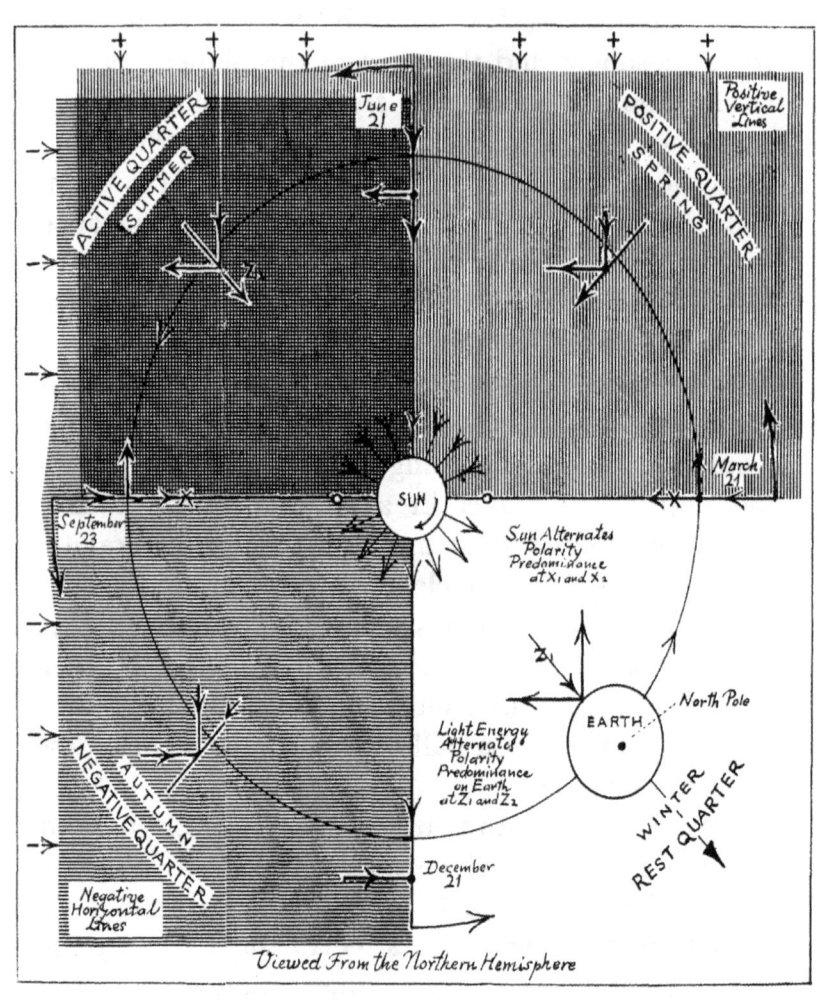

As the Sun crosses the Earth's Equator on March 21, it affects a positively charged cyclic predominance in the negative northern hemisphere.

In the arc from March 21 to September 23, the Sun tries to attract the Earth to it. This causes the negatively charged Earth to describe the arc of its orbit from March 21 to June 21. This is noted in the drawing as the Positive Quarter. The reason the Earth proceeds toward the negative lines of light energy in the Positive Quarter, is because the negative lines of light energy have been weakened from passing through the Sun's force field, or positively charged vortex.

As the Earth moves from June 21 to September 23, it starts in the downward direction of its elliptical arc. This is called the Active Quarter. These conditions are being viewed from the northern hemisphere in this explanation. In the southern hemisphere the Active and Rest Quarters would be opposite from those shown here.

As the negatively charged Earth follows its path in the Active Quarter, it is attracted by the positive Sun on the negative northern hemisphere and by the negative lines of light energy which are acting on the positive southern hemisphere. The positive lines of light energy are repelling on the positively predominant southern hemisphere.

The Active Quarter is Summer, our hottest season of the year. This heat is caused by the increase in resistance, set up gradually by the Sun extending its path on the Earth laterally to its northernmost extreme. In the daytime it is hotter because the Sun is farther into the negative northern hemisphere, thereby setting up more resistance in our negatively charged atmosphere and the negatively charged crust of the negative hemisphere. At the midway point between June 21 and September 23, the Earth also reaches its maximum exposure to the resistance of both the positive and negative lines of light energy. This increase in resistance from all three forces at the same time generates more heat.

As the Earth proceeds in its path from September 23 to December 21, the days become shorter as the Sun starts changing from the Equator into the positively charged southern hemisphere.

The positive Sun's effect on a positive hemisphere repels the planet. The negatively charged light lines of energy predominate and repel the planet from their direction of travel, causing it to arc through its orbit to December 21.

From December 21 to March 21 the negative predominance of the lines of light energy are again decreasing and at "Z" in the Rest Quarter all forces reach balance for an instant. At "Z" in the Rest Quarter the field or vortex of the Sun decreases both the positive and negative lines of light energy. The Sun has reached a half-way point between the Equator and its southernmost lateral extreme. Then the positive lines of light energy begin to attract the negatively charged planet and the increasing predominance of the negatively charged northern hemisphere. The Sun begins to attract the increasing negative predominance of the planet and the negative lines of light energy begin to repel the increasing negative predominance of the northern hemisphere.

The Sun and all of our planets are moving through space in the direction indicated by the arrow in the Rest Quarter of the drawing. Everything in the universe is trying to reach balance by traveling in the Rest Quarter direction.

The fact that the Earth has more land-mass in the northern hemisphere than in the southern hemisphere is the reason for the Earth's orbit being slightly elliptical. Land sets up more polarity action than water. The Sun acts upon the predominance of the polarity of the hemisphere presented to it by the Equinox alternation.

At March 21 and September 23, both the northern and the southern hemispheres are attracted and repelled equally and oppositely for an instant by the Sun.

The Sun reaches its maximum attraction on the Earth on June 21 and repels at its maximum on December 21.

The light lines of positive and negative energy act upon the Earth as an alternating, negatively charged body. The Sun acts upon the oppositely polarized hemispheres as they are presented to it in the seasons.

The relative increase or decrease in polarity action varies continuously, depending upon the tilt of the Earth, the resistance of the Sun's force field, and effects of the quarterly cycles upon each succeeding cycle.

People have less resistance to disease in Winter, because at that quarter of the Earth's orbit the life light lines of energy are reduced due to passing through the rotating vortex of the Sun's force field.

Any change of polarity predominance in the Earth's atmosphere or crust will result in climatic changes. This is how positively charged particles from Hydrogen bombs have caused weather changes and extremes throughout the world.

Our atmospheric strata is only a thin layer of gases and moisture emitted from the crust. Our frequent charging of the atmosphere with radioactive substances is a slow process of self-annihilation. The temperature drop noted after each atomic bomb blast is caused by the inrush of frigid air from higher strata. If 30 atomic bombs were exploded in 30 days, our Earth population would be forced underground by the extreme cold.

O man, I expand the buds in the springtime of My seasons. I bring forth hues of colors in the sunsets. I breathe forth fragrance from the flowers. I build a nest. I surge with Joy and Love, that you may grow in Unity and compassion. I bring about the warmth of My breath in the season of My summers, that man may know the fullness of the harvest, that man may see the repetition of My

PRODIGAL MOTHER

doings in examples all about him. And then I bring the cold, I change My colors. I cool My breath— the leaves of Me fall to nourish the soil, that once again I may come in the fullness of My springtime. And then I breathe My holy breath through naked branches in the blast of winter. I crown My mountains with the purity of whiteness, in mantles of snow. I freeze My rivers so that man may know the change that comes about in the seasons of My densities. I blast the breath of storm, and then I tire of cold and bring My seasons and cycles into repetition. My numberless worlds are there for man. The mysteries are there at hand to see, so man may know the Me in thee. When he solves the problems of My doing then I shall know he will grow in Me; he will know with Me—eternity.

This same principle of light energy maintains the Earth's cycles of day and night, temperature, tides, and the relation and effects of the Moon on the Earth and her people.

The Sun does not emit light of itself. The Sun transmits positively polarized force which reacts upon the Earth because of its negative polarity.

The Moon is one of the bodies acting as a governor to the Earth. The Earth's tides are a "fluid drive" connection between the motor-generator-battery Earth, and the governor Moon.

Gravity of the Moon has no effect upon the Earth. The only effect of the Moon upon the Earth is by polarity action on the Earth's force field, and by interruption of the light lines of force.

The Earth is surrounded by a self-generated force field. Nothing inside of the Earth's force field is affected by anything outside of it, except through the attracting or repelling effects of polarity in the lines of light energy, or the Sun.

Gravity within the force field generated by any body is not subject to the action of any body outside of the force field; unless the body outside of the force field is of opposite polarity.

The Moon and the Earth are both of negative polarity, as are all humans in their physical substance and all bodies that can be seen by reflected light.

All negative bodies generate a positive force field and all positively charged bodies generate a negative force field.

Temperature is the result of light forces acting in opposition to each other. Magnetism is an effect of primary light energy in opposition, produced as a result of its interruption by any body. Electricity is an effect of magnetism in polarity opposition. Heat is an effect of electricity in opposition. Contraction and expansion are opposite effects of heat, or the lack of it.

The Earth's force field is the boundary of everything inside of it. Nothing can come into it or go out through it without conforming to its positive polarity.

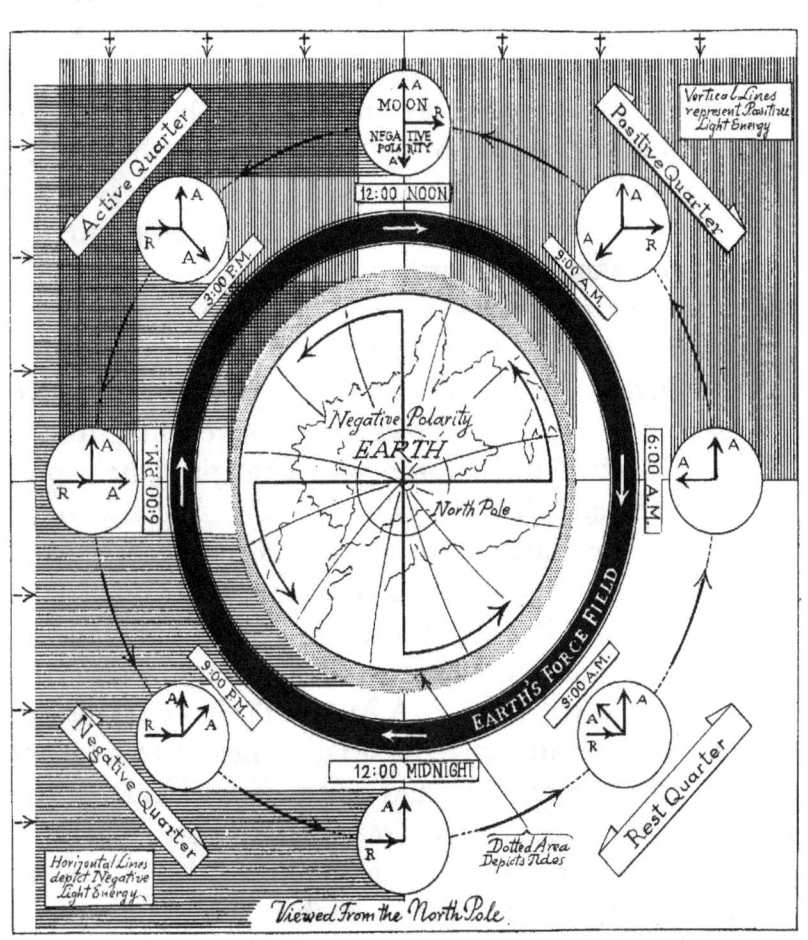

PRODIGAL MOTHER

The space people can alternate the polarity of the force field around their ships to conform to the positive polarity of the Earth's force field while they are passing through it.

The Moon never was hurled from the Earth and it will never be part of the Earth, due to the Earth's force field.

Let us start in the Positive Quarter and rotate the Moon around the Earth.

The small arrows shown on the Moon indicate the direction of forces set up by polarity affecting the Moon. The "A" arrows represent attractive forces and the "R" arrows stand for repelling forces. At all times these forces are changing their predominance, which establishes the Moon's orbit around the Earth. The Moon's orbit speed is fixed according to its charge of negative polarity.

The secondary light rays from the positive Sun and the positive lines of light energy warm the morning cycle from 6 A.M. to 12 Noon. This occurs by the attractive, resistance heat-effect in our negative atmosphere and crust of the Earth. The force field does not decrease these polarity effects because their polarities are both positive, therefore they offer no resistance to each other.

The heat registered during the hottest part of the day is in the Active Quarter from 12 Noon to 6 P.M. Higher temperatures are registered in this quarter because the Sun and positive lines of light energy are setting up attraction resistance within our atmosphere, and the negative lines of light energy are setting up repelling resistance. Two forces are working in attraction to the Earth's polarity and one force is working in opposition to it. The negative lines of force also meet resistance of the positive force field, which acts as a reflector.

From 6 P.M. to Midnight is the Negative Quarter. Both the positive lines of light energy and the Sun's attractive forces are eliminated and the negative lines of light energy maintain only the heat of resistance by repulsion. The forces of the Active Quarter fade away and the negative physical bodies of people become tired and sleepy during the Negative Quarter.

In the Rest Quarter from Midnight to 6 A.M., the Sun's positive force, the positive lines of light energy, and the negative lines of light energy set up no resistance of attractive or repelling forces. So the atmosphere and crust cool off in the coldest quarter of the cycle, because the Earth is shielded from the three forces. For the same reason more people die from "natural causes" in the Rest Quarter than in the other three quarters combined. This is because their "physical resistance" is low. In other words, none of the three life forces of light are active in the physical body during the Rest Quarter. That is what rest is—the lack of polarity opposition forces. Everything is meant to rest in the Rest Quarter and all of nature does it, except in cases where the positive polarity is predominant.

People of a prédominantly negative polarity cannot stand to work on a "graveyard shift". People of a predominantly positive polarity are often called lazy because their Active Quarter and Rest Quarter reactions are opposite and they want to sleep in the daytime.

It has been maintained by science that the Moon causes the tides. This is not so any more than the profession that heat comes from the Sun.

The polarity predominance alternates between the northern and southern hemispheres of the Earth and causes the force field to oscillate. The erratic orbit path of the Moon follows the oscillations of the Earth's force field. The Earth's positive force field rotates opposite to the Earth and the Moon's orbit. Interruptions of the light lines of force by other bodies or planets causes variable effects on the Earth and its reactions are transmitted to its self-generated force field.

The Earth's force field causes the tides, as it is of opposite polarity to the water. The fact that it is strongest at the point of most resistance—where the Moon is, explains the reason that science professes that the Moon attracts the water, causing the tides. A negative Moon cannot attract a negative body of water; it would repel the water and in that case the tides would be lowest on the Earth on the side toward the Moon.

The cyclic interruption by the Moon between the positive and negative lines of light energy and the Earth, is what causes diurnal inequalities in the four tides of a day and the age of the tide. Water being a fluid accounts for the equal effect on the opposite side of the Earth. The fact that the force field is rotating in the opposite direction to the Earth and is strongest at a point between the greatest resistance of attraction by both the Earth and the Moon, is what causes the "tides to lag"; a fact which has never been explained satisfactorily by science.

Magnetism in and around the Earth is a result of the Earth's interruption of the lines of primary light energy. Electricity is the result of interruption of the Earth's magnetism by a generator.

As the lines of primary light energy are in motion, any body that interrupts them will move according to its capacity and polarity charge.

Electricity is the second by-product of primary light energy; magnetism is the first. Neither can exist without the other because they are both part of each other.

In the drawing we show only the positively charged core of the Earth, the insulation, the negative crust, and the negative atmosphere. Actually these charged strata and insulating layers extend to strata around Mars and Venus.

The drawing is made with the Sun shining in the center of the Active Quarter from a 45° angle. The Sun is the alternator that changes polarity predominance from one hemisphere to the other every six months.

The "A" and "R" circles indicate the direction of the attracting and repelling forces. The negative primary light attracts the positive core in the Negative Quarter and repels the negative crust. The op-

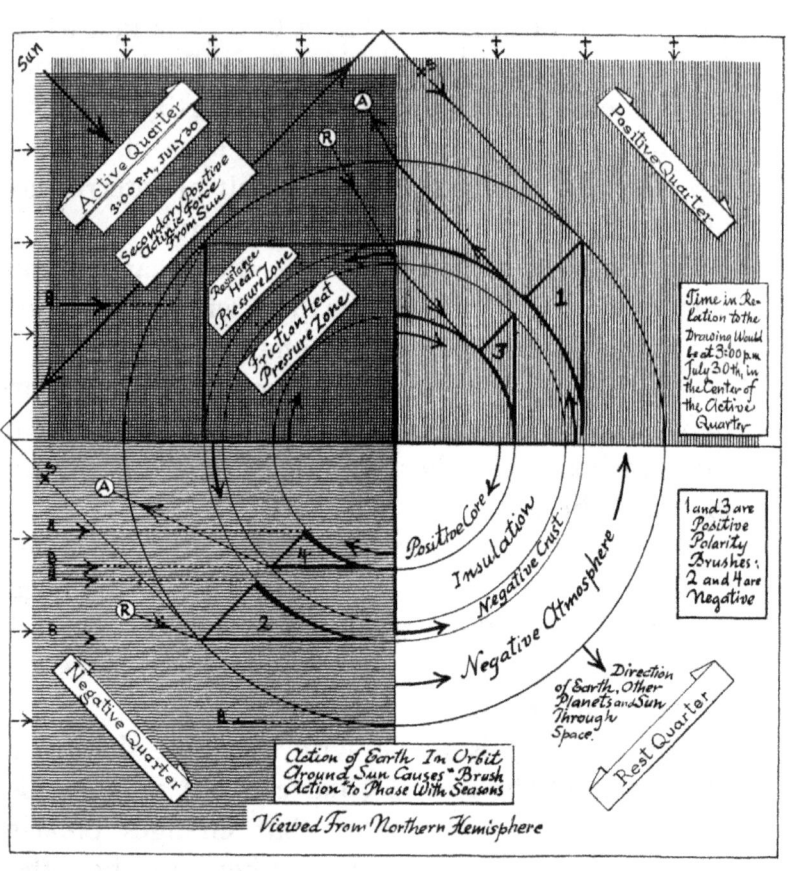

posite is true in the Positive Quarter. These attracting and repelling "brushes" are changing position continuously as the Earth orbits.

The atmosphere is actually a part of the crust and is of the same polarity. It acts as a bearing for the crust to turn in. The atmosphere and oceans are affected by the helical vortex set up in each hemisphere, which rotate in opposite directions. This is caused by the depleted lines of primary light giving their energy to cause motion of the planet. As they are depleted they try to reach rest, so they head for the points of least motion; which is at the poles. Naturally polarity seeks opposite polarity always.

A compass needle does not point to the north magnetic pole because it is attracted to it by an opposite polarity. Its negative charged end is only pressed into position parallel to the lines of light force going by it. The intelligence in the molecular arrangement of its negative charge wants to go with the other positively charged light lines in motion around it.

For the same reason the negative Earth, or our other planets were never part of the positive Sun. The planets being of opposite polarity could be attracted to it, but never thrown off from the Sun.

The Sun's insulation stratum prevents the positive polarity of the Sun from attracting the negative Earth into it.

Light is transmitted into energy by penetration into the matter that interrupts it. The matter then gains motion.

A negative vortex of light energy produces decelerating effects in negative matter. A positive vortex of light energy produces accelerating effects in negative matter.

You can apply the principle of the Earth's crust and core rotation in opposite directions to an electric motor.

Mount both ends of the shaft on fixed bearings. These bearings will suspend the entire motor.

Run the two wires from the motor case to two copper rings mounted on insulation, on one end of the shaft, inside the fixed bearing. Brushes from the power supply must contact the two rings.

Be sure to remove the base of the motor and balance the field case on the fixed bearings.

Power applied will rotate the armature in one direction and the field case in the other direction, at different speeds.

By applying a pulley to the shaft and another to the case, then running "V" belts from both pulleys to a common point of work, the torque force of the normal base type electric motor will also be applied to the work.

One "V" belt will have to be twisted 180 degrees between the motor pulley and the pulley of the work, to counteract the opposite rotations in the motor. This uses the torque force to do useful work, reduces speed and wear on the bearings, and furnishes more power for greater work output.

This is the same way the core and crust of the Earth function, *each being a balance to the other.*

The crust is the field and the core is the armature.

Unfortunately, the explosion of kiloton and megaton power "A" and "H" bombs have unbalanced natural conditions. This will bring about a steady increase in subterranean temperatures in the northern hemisphere, and lowering of temperatures in the southern hemisphere. The rapid shifting of the magnetic poles registered on the surface is the result of these bombs unbalancing the planet. Wherever the magnetic poles on the negative polarity surface are found, *they indicate where the axis of the positive polarity core is located under the crust.*

The core is encased in fluid obsidian 600 miles thick. Oscillations of the core, which were set up by the reaction to the bomb forces, will cause an increase in volcanoes and earthquakes, due to increased frictional heat in the fluid separator.

Throw the fine balance of the electric motor case out, and see what would happen to the armature if it were floating in a fluid. Any spinning gyroscope will wobble if it is moved from its plane of rotation. The Earth works like a gyroscope.

Magnets, atoms, planets, and people all have polarities of either positive, or negative predominance.

Because a body predominates in one polarity does not mean that the substance of its composition does not include matter of the opposite polarity.

When your positive polarity body reaches predominance your negative polarity physical body dies.

The same thing applies to planets, magnets, or atomic structure.

The nuclear (positive polarity) devices being exploded in our negative polarity atmosphere are rapidly bringing about a condition of polar change on the Earth's surface. The emission of positive polarity particles (fallout) from the "H" bomb tests are unbalancing the polarity predominance of the Earth.

The positive fallout particles are attracted to the negative polarity, north magnetic pole. When the positive particles fall there on negative polarity ice the resistance causes heat, causing the ice to melt.

The negative polarity water released by melting is repelled by the more predominantly negative polarity crust of the Earth into a less predominantly negative polarity atmosphere.

In the air it is attracted in a spiral course to the positively predominant southern hemisphere, where most of it is attracted to the positive polarity, south magnetic pole.

This causes ice to build up at the southern pole and melt at the northern pole, bringing unbalance to the planet's axis indirectly from the explosion of nuclear bombs.

The magnetic poles registered on the surface of the Earth's crust are in reality the axis poles of the Earth's positive polarity core. As more bomb tests transmute negative polarity matter to a positive polarity condition, the effects can be registered in many ways.

The magnetic declination shown on the Los Angeles (R-2) Sectional Aeronautical Chart, dated March 10, 1953, shows the 15° E. magnetic declination line at 115° 50′ W. Longitude at the 34° N. Latitude line. The chart dated September 27, 1955, shows a shift of the 15° E. magnetic declination to 117° 2′ W. This is a change of 1° 12′ in 2½ years, or 28.8′ per year. Formerly it was slightly over 9′ per year.

The main reason for low layers of smog over most of the big cities is because the carbon particles in the air are not repelled upward as they used to be before the advent of "H" bomb tests. The polarity of these particles normally being negative, they are becoming less negative due to the fact that carbon assimilates radioactivity of positive polarity; thus the repelling action is reduced and the particles hang closer to the surface instead of rising to be dispersed by the winds at higher altitudes.

Magnetism is the positive and negative fields generated by the revolving planet interrupting the positive and negative lines of primary energy present in all space. Electricity is the force generated by an armature interrupting the positive and negative lines of magnetism. Each has its effect on the other, and can be converted into the other.

The "time" field separates all primary polarities, all magnetic polarities, and all electrical polarities. This "time" field is unseen, infinite, and maintains the balance between the opposite charges present

THE COUNCIL OF SEVEN LIGHTS

in all bodies. This balance is manifest in all new creations.

With the continual testing of nuclear devices the planet's unbalance will increase by the equal and opposite reaction of polarities coming ever closer to balance.

This will bring about more ionization of the atmosphere, with an increase in smog, humidity, and clouds. Then the Bible prophecy will be fulfilled that says, "The Sun will no longer give forth her light".

In the pattern of My ways I live My life in many forms, known and unknown to other parts of Me. I live in space of Me to constantly supervise My doings; I live in soil to nourish My roots. I am the sap, the blood; in every density I am. I live My life and love it too, being the living Love of you, thrilling when you express the Me in thee.

My life is sad only when you are mad at other parts of Me. Only when you manifest hate to destroy; then I wait patiently for you to recover, to discover that you have only injured Me and thee.

Your every fight is My fight too, but not when it is aimed at other beings of Me. Your fight is to overcome the urge; to purge yourself of war and woe. None can hold to Me and proclaim victory over others of My parts as foe. I am here and there, and everywhere. Justice is fair play with Me and Mine in My eternity of now.

The "New Jerusalem" referred to in the Bible, in Rev. 21:10, is not really new. It is the positive polarity "moon" that has been orbiting around the Earth for many thousands of years.

This satellite, called "Shanchea" by the space people, is a spacecraft. Their name for the Earth is "Shan". "Chea" means child in their language of the Solex-Mal, or Solar Tongue. Therefore the name of this ship is "Earthchild" in English. This same craft was called the "Star of Bethlehem" over nineteen hundred years ago at the birth of the child called Jesus.

This positive polarity spaceship is square. This is not new information. It has been before our eyes hundreds of years in print; though it was not recognized. Rev. 21:16 tells you, "And the city lieth foursquare, and the length is as large as the breadth: and he measured the city with the reed, twelve thousand furlongs. The length and the breadth and the height of it are equal."

The reason it was called "The Star of Bethlehem" was because when it is activated under control it looks like a star to physical vision. The last time its power units were activated was when the man Jesus was "born". This "positive star body" generates a negative force field around it to protect it when it is in motion as a ship.

"Beth" is used today as "Beta", meaning negative. "Le" is used today as "lea", meaning a meadow. "Hem" can be understood by any woman as the thing that goes around the bottom of a dress. "Star

THE COUNCIL OF SEVEN LIGHTS

of Beta-le-hem" means a positive body, with a negative force field around it, over a meadow. That is where Jesus was born—in a manger, in a meadow.

Shanchea is orbiting around the Earth in the Earth's positive force field. It cannot be seen by telescopes because it sets up no resistance to the Sun's positive rays.

The Bible tells further, in Rev. 21:11; "Having the glory of God: and her light was like unto a stone most precious, even like jasper stone, *clear as a crystal.*"

The "Seven Lights" are spoken of in Rev. 1:20; "The mystery of the *seven stars* which thou sawest in my right hand (positive polarity), and the seven golden candlesticks. The *seven stars* are the angels (space people) of the seven churches (seven levels of life around the Earth): and the seven candlesticks which thou sawest are the seven churches."

The population of this level of life on the Earth is composed of people from the other six levels. Chapters 2 and 3 of Revelations tells which of the levels you are from. One of these seven church descriptions fits every mortal in this level.

The population of Shanchea is given in Rev. 5:11; "And I beheld, and I heard the voice of many angels round the throne and the beasts and the elders: and the number of them was *ten thousand times ten thousand, and thousands of thousands.*"

THE COUNCIL OF SEVEN LIGHTS

I am the voice, O mortal man, that whispers in the silence of your Being. I am the motion, instilled within the fluid dust of the body, to encase you in this density of three. I am the softness that all babes know when nestled to the breast of Me. I am the hardness of the substance many times beyond the density that mortals know. I am the sun that warms the morn', and scorches brow. For thou must know, within the Being of Me is thee. And search, though you may do for eons yet to come, I am not there where you may go. I am within you giving Life to clay, that My motion may be manifest for purposes misunderstood by man. I am not the formula of many, nor of one, My combination varies with each speck of dust, with each drop of rain, with each thought, each individual pain and hope. For I am always surrounding thee, and thee in Me but makes the journey short. Look not afar, look where you are—eternity is Now!

O man, you need not chart a roadway through the stars to Me. You need not cross the land, or search beyond the sea. You will find Me in the smile, in the look of someone you have helped along the way. You only have to search your heart and start to find that I am there—wherever you may be. Though all the roads may lead to me; though many search eternally to find a shortcut in the way— I am there and here, as close as you to Me. So reach not for a star afar, search not in the distance, in the future, or the past. At last you are aware that I am there within your Being, watching how you treat the Me in others of My parts.

CHAPTER EIGHT

METHUSELAH'S TOY

The Great Pyramid ("Pyr" means Fire; "Mid", the equal distance between the extremes; PYRAMID: Fire, or positive light substance in the middle) of Gizeh, Egypt, is the only existant structure on the Earth that remains intact after 25,816 years. It is the greatest power plant ever built on this planet. At the time of its use it could furnish more power than the generators at Niagara Falls could produce in a thousand years.

The Great Pyramid was never intended to be a tomb or a monument for the Pharaohs. Neither was it built by the Egyptians or Hyksos, as assumed by historians. It was erected by a remnant of the Adamic race on this planet.

In order to produce the power required, the Pyramid was built in minute conformity to the measurements of our solar system. All dimensions were accurately computed to insure correct functional operation.

The Pyramid was designed by Enoch and built by Thothma with the help of the true descendants of the Adamic race (the space people) who had made a forced landing on Earth. Knowing the Universal Laws and their application they received timely warning and journeyed to Egypt before the sinking of the great continent Atlantis—Enoch and

THE COUNCIL OF SEVEN LIGHTS

Thothma flying in an aircraft called "vailx". After landing in Egypt 25,825 years ago, they started the operations and spent the next nine years in building the Great Pyramid.

Utilizing knowledge gleaned from their secret records, they employed the infinite Light powers. They knew how to manipulate the light lines of force to cut the blocks with light energy from the "A" positive and "B" negative lines of force. They transported the heavy blocks with their vailx. Hovering over each block they encompassed it in their force field, eliminating the weight of the block in relation to the Earth. The blocks shaped so as to assure astronomical precision, correspond to and contain all pertinent data of our Earth and solar system. These correct dimensions were necessary in creating a positive solar vortex—on a small scale—from the "A" positive and "B" negative lines of light force.

The Great Pyramid was erected at its present location for several reasons. Its location was on the side of the negative polarity from the Equator. The 30° latitude was the maximum vortex belt on both sides of the Equator. It was lateral through the Earth to the positive pole of the planet's core. It was centrally located on the Earth's land-mass, which was its nearest maximum point of negative polarity. It was opposite to the Earth's largest mass of water, which served as a reflector.

The weight of the Pyramid had to be tremendous in order to prevent its twisting out of shape, or rotating on its base. The controversial capstone and

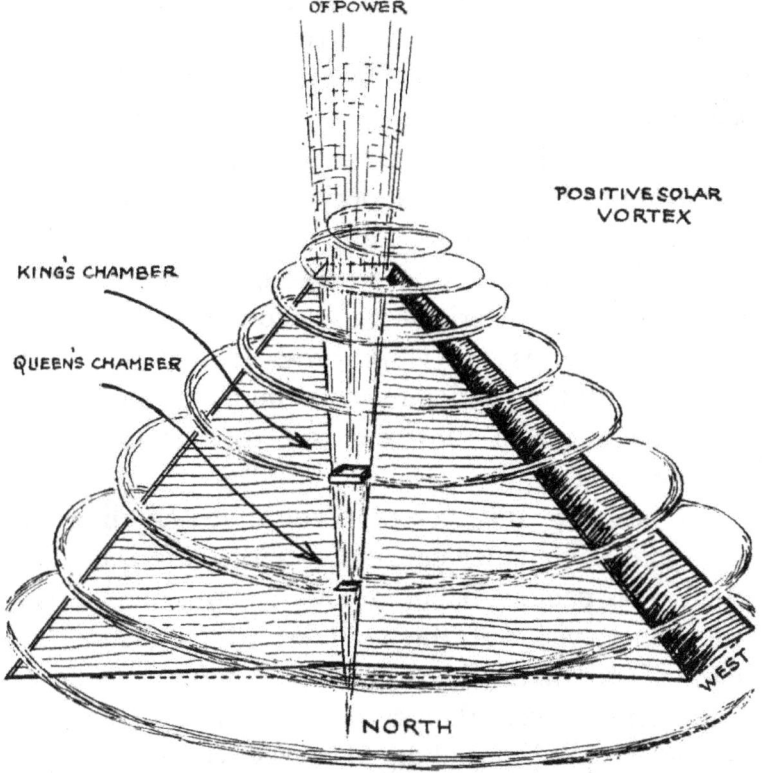

B⁻ lines of force. They transported the heavy blocks with their vailx (a model T version of the spacecraft now in our atmosphere). Hovering over each block they encompassed it in their force field, eliminating the weight of the block in relation to the Earth. The blocks shaped so in completeness, as to assure astronomical precision, correspond to and contain all pertinent data of our Earth and Solar System. These correct dimensions were necessary in creating a positive solar vortex on a small scale — from the A⁺ and B⁻ lines of light force.

a few courses of blocks were left off intentionally, as experiments proved they were not needed.

As the Earth rotated, each revolution brought the Pyramid into a cycle of "A" positive and "B" negative lines of force. This caused an increase in the vortex-shaft of positive force (the principle of the cyclotron). Thus after a period of days the vortex reached and held its maximum force.

All this planning and work—astronomy, mathematics and engineering—was recorded symbolically in the stones as the work progressed. Jesus knew this by intuition and journeyed to Egypt to refresh his memory from the stone-records erected by his people.

In building this power plant of astounding dimensions their chief concern was the safe return to their own people. Being endowed with true perception, they visioned the coming cataclysms of the planet and planned an exodus. When the time of departure arrived, they entered the King's Chamber in the Pyramid and charged themselves in the super light-force vortex. Then they boarded their ships, hovering for a while over the truncated top of the Pyramid in the positive shaft of force which extended beyond the gravity range of the planet. When the ships were properly charged they were actually repelled from the planet and navigated with super speed to their destination.

Some of the sons of God (the Adamic race), who remained on this planet, knew of and used the stored-up power of the Pyramid for several thousand years. For instance, Methuselah and his sons prolonged their life span for hundreds of years by charging their bodies in the vortex. Many of the deceased Pharaohs, placed in the "open tomb" of the King's Chamber for regeneration, were restored to life. Those who did not revive were left there for a period of 28 days, during which time the mummification took place.

However, as the Earth moved in the Precession of the Equinox the regenerative and rejuvenating powers embodied in the Pyramid were lost. Rulers around the Earth, knowing of the rejuvenating powers of the pyramid, tried to duplicate the Great Pyramid of Gizeh by building a pyramid of their own by manual labor in order to live longer themselves. They did not fully know the principles of primary energy however, so their pyramids became their tombs. Nevertheless, the secrets are not completely lost.

Humans, knowing they are alive now, and not knowing what lies beyond the transition called death, attempt by every means possible to keep their physical bodies alive.

The inner mind keeps transmitting the faint hope to their understanding that they can live forever. Naturally, knowing that they possess a physical vehicle now, they are reluctant to part with the old model to which they have become accustomed.

Monkey glands, hormones, operations, injections, etc., have been advanced by the technicians in biological and medical science to try to prolong the life of the physical body. People assume that substance of a physical or chemical nature can support substance of like physical nature. This is based on the theory that if you keep adding dirt to a hill that erosion is constantly dispersing, it will always be a hill. Nature always wins the battle in the long run, because natural forces are eternal. Man's efforts to overcome nature *by opposing it* will lose every time. The *only* means by which man can add years to the physical form is by *going with* the natural, eternal forces.

Life is eternally continuous. Humans have placed the limits of *was, are,* and *will be* on life. These divisions of time are from the physical brain. The flesh we call the brain only *understands now*, it only exists in the physical body for *now*. It cannot understand anything beyond its own limits of birth and death. All physical substance changes in time.

It is understandable when one has spent his years in building up associations, friends, and family, why he wishes to remain here longer. His brain concept of the physical body does not want to give up its encasing form.

The biggest trouble on this planet is, that when you get smart enough to do something with the knowledge you have acquired here, death intervenes. Our life span is just too short.

In Genesis, chapter 5, it tells of Seth, Enos, Jared, Methuselah, and others living for hundreds of years. They were so close to the knowledge of their ancestors of the Adamic colony on Earth, that they

METHUSELAH'S TOY

used the "fountain of youth" principles to add to their lifespan.

Rejuvenation is done with the infinite light, or what is called "God power". In the application of this power the one receiving it does not see, feel, taste, smell, or hear anything. I have the information to make rejuvenation possible; adding 50 to 80 year onto the average lifespan *plus* resumption of youthful vitality.

The only difficulty I will have, is that we are on a planet that is revolving. In order to operate this apparatus I must clock it to the Earth's rotation, quite like a large telescope is clocked to keep it centered on the object being viewed.

THE COUNCIL OF SEVEN LIGHTS

O mortal beings, though many may express belief in the teachers I have sent, I accept them, providing that the expression of belief is not a living lie. And those who live My Laws and say "There is no God above", them I accept also. Though words may deny My person, the actions prove Me in the heart. Belief expressed in words is not verified in fact unless the living brings about the proof.

Though multitudes have closed the door that keeps Me from being the directing force, I condemn them not. Though Laws may make My Being infinite and boundless beyond comprehension, I am not there in the individual except as I am expressed in action.

O mortals bound in density, look to the examples I have placed around you. Bow not your head to come to Me, only prepare that I may be recognized within your Being. Stumble not on barriers that mortal eyes fail to see. Build the perception within that may guide your path, that I may light the way so none shall stumble in progress of eternity. Lean not upon the cane of chance, but only cast a glance in My direction, which is within, to find the way by day or night. I make the path, I light the light. I lead you by the hand and yet you trust Me not, although you profess My Being in words. The cycle has come in the circulation of My doing, and now I lead My faithful ones to victory over self. For they shall recognize My Image is the light of sight, the light of right, instilled within each of My parts.

THE COUNCIL OF SEVEN LIGHTS

And though I shake the ashes of My universe, the furnaces of My heat shall ever be—the Love of Me expressed in thee.

Chapter Nine

THE SWORD OF DAMOCLES

I have explained that nearly everyone on this old Earth has the more or less dormant potential to communicate by thought. Like learning to play the piano, or learning to become a master of any trade, sport, or other activity, the use of thought communication can only be accomplished by regular, continuous practice.

The space people use instrumentation in their thought contacts with people, only to insure positive reception and to maintain power through conditions that could otherwise interrupt the reception.

They think into a device they call an "adiphon". This receiver in turn transmits through a projector they call an "omnibeam". The "omnibeam" can be focused on any individual, or a group of people. This projecting of thoughts is mentioned throughout the Bible. Voices "coming from heaven". The "Lord" speaking unto Moses and many others, including the voice of God coming to Jesus.

The space people have explained that they can only focus this beam *safely* on people who have devoted much time to an awareness of "open" perception. Otherwise, the beam can be dangerous to the physical health of anyone that cannot stand its powerful vibratory transmission.

One person has the power of *one* and can nor-

THE SWORD OF DAMOCLES

mally only contact one other individual. Here on the Earth one power of thought is sufficient in the Earth's magnetic field to contact any one other individual who is receptive at the time, anywhere on the Earth's surface.

Thought projection by one person must be done by concentrating upon the individual you wish to receive your thought. Thinking his name, and what he looks like, must be pictured in the projector's mind several times. Then the thought you wish to transmit must be concentrated upon several times. This is for beginners. After one becomes adept at projection, only one thought, person, picture, in the projector's mind will be necessary.

The thought will not be projected to the one of whom you are thinking until you release the thought. In other words, after the concentration you must immediately forget what you were projecting and think of anything else. As long as you hold the thought in your mind it will not reach the one you are projecting to.

Unless the person you are projecting to is in a receptive state, he may not receive the thought. To be receptive you must make your mind a blank. Do not think of anything while trying to receive the thoughts of others.

With continuous practice your projective and receptive ability will become apparent to you.

The power of thought can be increased by the increase in the number of people. One person has one power. Two people have eight power. Three people have 512 power. This power cubes its resultant to the maximum of twelve people.

This is the formula Jesus gave to the people when the Creative Spirit spoke through him, saying; "When *two or more* are gathered in My name there am I also".

This is the force that the Supreme Intelligence used to think the universe into being. Nothing can be manifested without first being thought of by someone.

As I have said, three people have the projective force of 512 power. Four people increase it to 134,-217,728 power. When twelve people combine their thought force in unity, on *any* purpose, that purpose would be accomplished.

This is the reason Jesus did not select his disciples from among the intellectuals of his day. He would have had too many fixed ideas to undo in their minds. Instead, he picked common people from among the multitudes, only one of which could even write. He knew that it would be easier to use the power of twelve simple-minded people than to undo the dogma, custom, and religious illusions established in the minds of the "learned".

Most of the acts Jesus performed were done through the concentrated power of his twelve disciples, with Jesus controlling this tremendous power. These acts have been termed miracles by people who didn't understand them. *There are no miracles.* Everything comes about by the natural laws of cause and effect. Thought is the causal force of all effects.

THE SWORD OF DAMOCLES

Thought is of positive polarity predominance, as it is a causal, or projective force. In the physical level of negative polarity predominance, thought cannot manifest by itself.

Polarity requires that two poles be active to manifest a result. A battery with only a positive pole will not produce current. Duality is required in equal and opposite forces in order to manifest action as the resultant.

Motion can only be when unbalance exists. That which is in balance cannot move of itself. Some other force must cause the action. This is why the expression of "God helps those that help themselves" is a universal law.

The Bible tells you that "God rested on the seventh day." Nowhere does it tell you that God started creating again. It says that God completed His works. This means that God is still resting, and can only be manifested through man, who was given dominion over all things. This in itself is proof of reincarnation. God made the race of man and then rested. Everyone of the race of man was created simultaneously. No one is older, or younger, than another. When God rested, creation was terminated by God. Birth of babies on the Earth is only the repetition of their eternal creation here, or somewhere else in the universe, before.

Death is only the departure from negative polarity manifestation to positive polarity manifestation. Life is only manifested through the interchange of motion through the unbalanced opposites.

THE COUNCIL OF SEVEN LIGHTS

God is *no*-thing. If God were a thing, God would have individuality and could not be infinite, for individuality is only a part of everything. God is referred to as He, the Father, etc., by the church. This nullifies God's infinity and gives male gender to God. This excludes everything feminine and of negative polarity. The church would have God in the image of man, rather than man in the image of God.

To use God power, you must bring it out of stillness and manifest It through expression, or motion, to produce a given result. In giving man dominion over all things except his fellow men, God expected you to use the infinite Intelligence of universal Being to manifest results.

Why did Jesus say he came to bring the Word? He could have easily communicated with anyone he wanted to by thought, but he said he came to bring the *Word*.

The reason was that he knew the power of God (Rest) could only be manifested in a predominately negative polarity level of life by an equal interchange of thought (positive polarity) and expression (negative polarity).

It is not my intention to prove this formula to you, but rather to let your reason and experiences prove it to yourself. Look back through your experiences and recall if the following has happened to you before. Apply it now and make it work now. God's power has no limits except those that man creates.

Think regularly every night between 6 P.M. and Midnight of something you *need*. This is projecting

THE SWORD OF DAMOCLES

positive thought, by concentration, into the negative polarity (receptive) lines of force, which alone are active in this quarter of the twenty-four hour rotation of the Earth.

Then during the time from 6 A.M. to Noon, which is the positive quarter relative to the projective, positive polarity lines of force, express in *words* that you *do not want* the things you thought about during the 6 P.M. to Midnight quarter.

By attraction, positive thought to negative force and negative expression (the word) to positive force, you can receive that which you have put the forces of the universe in motion for.

This should be done regularly, night and morning, for 28 consecutive days (one magnetic month), and then release it by forgetting *entirely* about it.

This can be used for others, especially if you *do not tell* them what you are doing for them. Telling them will bring their mind action into play and will interfere with the results.

Once this formula is applied exactly *as given,* nothing in the universe can prevent the results from manifesting.

You must *think* what you *need,* or others *need,* and use "The Word" or the power of opposite polarity, and patiently wait for the result after forgetting about it or releasing it into God's hands.

The Creator caused the universe to be. Then all was given unto the dominion of Man throughout the universe.

Man, using the force of thought, can create new

things for progression, or create new things for destruction. Thought is the prime force and is neutral.

Words are the effect of thoughts, whether they be good or bad. Words are in the range of our physical hearing. They are the means by which thoughts are conveyed between people with sound. Various languages convey the same meaning by different sounds.

There have been many arguments, discussions, and efforts to prove that things, and people, not seen in our life level, can be materialized. The Bible tells many times about "angels" appearing before people, apparently out of thin air.

To believe in the Bible of Christianity, with the concept that "angels" appeared in olden time, and cannot appear in our time; is certainly bullheaded orthodoxy. This is primarily done by some "Christians" who do no want "angels" to interfere with their selfish ways and pleasures.

Much has been said about the space people of today materializing and de-materializing on several occasions. I can truthfully say that I have seen and talked with one of them that instantly disappeared to my vision; but I could still feel him when I touched where I had just seen him.

Just as orthodoxy places limits on people's thinking, so does your physical sense of sight place limits on your seeing. Your eyes can only see within the range of the visible spectrum; about 4000 to 7800 Angstroms in wave length measurement.

You cannot see the air, yet you breathe it. You can see water in its fluid density and its vaporous density, but when the steam is absorbed in the air, you cannot see it.

Vibrations from about 20 to nearly 20,000 cycles a second can be heard with the ears. Vibrations below our hearing level are called "infrasonic" and those above it "ultrasonic".

Because the five lower senses all have limits, people's thinking has become narrowed into a groove that will not allow them to accept anything that is not within their limitations.

Many of the space people live in frequencies of life beyond the human limits. By using methods developed by them, they can bring their body vibrations inside our visual limits as easily as we can condense unseen moisture out of the air into water, and then freeze it into ice.

Many spiritualist mediums can materialize people from beyond the door of death. Do not let yourself be confused, however, with these ectoplasmic figures, or the words spoken through them. All figures of people generated through the ectoplasm of another person are from the transition or Earthbound level, or are created from the mind of the medium.

This is not to be scoffed at, as the power to create from the mind is a great one indeed. *None* of the space people from other levels of life are ever materialized through a medium. It is not possible to bring through ectoplasmic means, anyone from beyond the Earth's force field.

In order to progress to the finer frequencies of life in other levels, you must first know where you stand in this level. The Creative Spirit so designed His light universe that nothing can exceed its individual vibratory qualifications.

Your individual record is being made daily by the way you live. Everything you think, say, or do is recorded in your aura. In the life following this one, you will only be able to progress to the highest level in which your light record will vibrate. No one is going to judge you but yourself, and you will be faced with the results of the record you established here.

You must conform in the way you live to the laws of the universe. The densities are established by different vibratory frequencies of light. You can qualify to "jump grades" by the way you live here now.

THE COUNCIL OF SEVEN LIGHTS

I am the voice, O man, speaking in the stillness of your Being. The righteous recognize My voice. My call is to those whose ears are deaf to My withinness. I plead eternally, that all may hear the Me in you eventually. In the pattern of My doings I bring you pain and joy, that you may feel Me in the contrast of your senses. Never shall I cease to call to those who live in darkness. Though My patience is infinite, I suffer because of your sins. When you hear Me in another—listen! Do not shy from Me in the disguise of raucous laughter. The ones who live in the clamor of confusion, to hide from Me, are only adding sorrow to tomorrow. So I make each tomorrow a today, that your memory of yesterday shall make My voice the louder from out of the silence of an added day you spent alone.

I have extended the Light to manifest My creations from thought of Me, and perpetuated motion throughout eternity. Each motion to bring an effect, and every effect a cause—by repetition—in an endless pattern of My doings.

I ended My work of bringing about, and made thee, O man, to carry continuity. My infinite watching is directed to see My Image of instrumentality, which is thee, O man.

Whenever you sing—My heart sings too, through joy of your emotion. And when you assist another— the act of thee is devotion to Me, and from Me through thee.

Whenever you sorrow, I am sad too; each thrill you feel is transmitted to Me. I too am ignored when you fail to see the Me in others around you. Though you are effect of My cause, O man— Intelligent Image of Me—I only exist as effect of you whenever you cause Me to be an extension through thee. Then am I active, then do I live, when you give effect to My cause in the love of Me—through each day of My days, eternally.

CHAPTER TEN

THE FALSE CHARIOT

You must understand that the substance you call your body is very much like the body of an automobile. The chassis on which the substance forms is the eternal part of you. You can lose a limb or smash the body and the chassis of your Reality continues on. In physical level requirements, your material body is of an animal structure following the form of eternal man in the essence of your real Self. This material structure is given life by the fact that the *forms of crystals* within the blood stream are the power house of your every motion.

These microscopic crystals in the blood diffuse, refract, and reflect the positive-negative light passing through you continuously. These crystals often become neutral. They lose their power, like a magnet. Each of these crystals is polarized and carries polarity in opposition. This brings about the flow of your blood through light energy. Many times as these crystals neutralize, they will settle in the feet. This is the reason for the ancient teachings concerning the position of standing on the head—to circulate these crystals that have become neutral.

The heart is caused to function by the circulation of the blood, instead of vice-versa. The heart serves only as a valve to keep the circulation going in one direction. The structure of arteries is such that the cellular and atomic composition brings about a positive force upon the crystals in the blood stream. The veins are such that negative force of light energy functions through them. Being of animal structure, man in the physical body requires *crystals of an animal nature*. Various refractory crystals found in animal foods are *not reproduced by vegetation*.

The history of the mechanics of motion throughout the universe is locked in crystals. The records of all that is, all that was, and ever shall be are concealed in the frequencies of various elements known and unknown in their crystal perfection. Life is only given motion through various particles of matter in many forms. As the Bible tells you "the blood is the life". It transmits and circulates light energy into substance form of animal nature, which conforms to the pattern of man's real form.

The flesh fills the real body, although the real body extends beyond the skin boundaries of the physical.

As you are born in this form, called the physical body, your instant beginning in this level was brought here in the seed, or the control master cell, through the infinite "G" line of light force. This control master cell was the beginning of your physical body.

Under the functions of the control master cell, there are many other master cells. These master cells compose each one a center, the beginning of your vital organs and glands. The brain is a gland.

The control master cell is the essence of form. It is subject to absorption of characteristics from both the male and female parents. The consciousness of Being is the center of the control master cell, maintaining the records of all previous lives and experiènces in other levels.

As these cells grow, bringing from a seed the form, controlled by the absorption of the control master cell, each child is endowed with good and bad traits of both parents. The seed which came over the infinite line of force contained none of the parent's characteristics.

As this control master cell gives instructions, each master cell comes to attention in the proper position in the body, like a well regimented army, all officers. Each of these officer master cells gathers recruits from the atomic substances in the "A" and "B" lines of force and develops each their own individual portion of the physical body. This continues until so-called "death" on this level.

Roughly every seven years these master cell intelligences, centering the organs and glands, are relieved by other officers. Roughly every 28 years, the control master cell is relieved by another; better qualified in more mature lines. The secret of long life is in the ability, through consciousness, to control the change of these control master cells.

Some people have assumed that the mind of individuals is in the head, because through progressive conditioning they have been led to believe that the brain is the control of the mind. The mind is infinite and universal. The mind is not confined within the body.

THE COUNCIL OF SEVEN LIGHTS

In observing with the third eye, or the consciousness of your positive polarity vision, do not assume that the ability of this particular awareness is located anywhere within the physical body. Those whose concept of this vision is from the pineal gland area, will naturally seem to focus in that area. Actually your consciousness of individual being is all over your body, and in any particular experience is concentrated at the point of greatest sensation.

If you smash a toe and the toe hurts, that is the point at which your greatest concentration of consciousness is recorded.

The consciousness of your individual being moves with your emotions. It flares with various ones of these emotions, and recedes with others.

Mind, being universal, is all through you and you are in it. Your consciousness is the doorway to Universal Mind.

The scope of your consciousness can be increased with practice. Because you observe ahead of you with your negative polarity, physical vision, you assume to look ahead of you with your inner vision. This is limiting your scope.

A particular time to practice the expansion of your consciousness awareness is when you retire at night. When you close your eyes, do not attempt to concentrate a light, or your positive vision, at the center of the forehead. Attempt to penetrate into the blackness, into the depths, with your projective inner vision. Look into the darkness. Focus deeply and further away.

THE FALSE CHARIOT

It is possible with practice to focus your inner vision as you do your physical vision. Attempt to extend your inner vision. Penetrate further and further each night into the darkness.

If you are outside observing the stars, try to look beyond the stars. In the spaces between them attempt to see another star where none can be seen with your limited physical vision. This practice with the physical vision will also expand the inner vision.

With constant and regular practice you should be able, within a six month's period, to throw the limits of your forward vision out. You should expand your inner vision to cover three hundred and sixty degrees and see as well behind as ahead, or to either side. The limits of your forward physical vision are not applicable to the inner vision.

The nightly practice will reveal to you that many things are within the scope of your inner vision, and your mind concept enlarges. Your consciousness penetrates with your attempt to extend your inner vision, and you grasp more of what mind is.

What is life? What is light? Who is God? Where is heaven? These and many other questions are asked by numerous people daily. Wherever there is Life there is Light, and wherever there is Light there is God.

Orthodoxy preaches that God is of male gender, saying He or Him. This implication gives to the Creator sex. The Single One is an "ity", composed of uncountable entities. The Creator is a power of Infinite, Boundless, Eternity. Wherever Life manifests motion, there is Soul in polarity opposition. Wherever Life manifests motion and consciousness, there is Spirit-Intelligence present as a part of the Creative Mind. Dimensional aspects of individuals in densities, leads to spiral inclinations of finer levels of life. You are all sitting in God, breathing God in, and He is manifesting Life in physical form through His right hand of positive polarity and His left hand of negative polarity. In-between the uncountable billions of lines of light energy passing through you, there *scientifically* is God; insulating the oppositely polarized light energies from each other. Centering your consciousness individually, there is the staff of Light and Life eternal.

Though God is still, the opposite light energies are in motion. When you move any muscle, light energy is the motive power. Light energy functions through the Spirit. The Single One is Universal Spirit—unseen, potent, supreme Intelligence, composed of innumerable individual minds. When you record through any sense of smell, touch, taste, sight, hearing, thought, or Being, it is the spirit of you that records the action. The substance of flesh is inert to sensing. The conscious mind of God is yours to use, like a universal library; but each must enter through his individual door to read the records.

Mundane philosophies, scientific theories, or religious beliefs do not serve as keys to enter God's house. You each must individually open your own door and when you do, you will discover first that you were inside all the time, but were not aware of it.

THE FALSE CHARIOT

Few people who attend church understand the beginning of the church. The church buildings today are patterned after an ancient worship.

Man and woman originally assumed they had reached a state of being part of God, in the ultimate in the physical body, when the woman gave birth to a child. The man and the woman considered they had performed a creative act. This is the primary urge of all creation, to recreate. The understanding of the people was, that two things entered into the act of recreation. The male and female were essential to birth.

In the time of the ancients, religious worship was conducted in the open. The ancient rites were conducted where a large rock pointed heavenward, symbolizing the projective male; and where another rock presented a cleavage, representing the female.

These phallic rites were conducted in reverence, although modern history would lead us to believe that they were sex orgies. The rites were worship in the most sincere form.

The church buildings today still present the spire to heaven as the symbol of the projective male. The double open doors still represent the cleavage, the receptive opening of the female.

Modern society does not understand sex and its relation to religion. *They cannot be separated.*

The act of bringing a child to birth is not the part of the parent's choice. It is the choice of the child that brings it to birth through the parents. Although many would try to prevent having children, those who are qualified will have children in spite of themselves.

Throughout history, sex has been mentioned more than any other subject. The Bible is full of it. Everyone wants to be in on the act because it is the natural, conductive method of recreation.

Naturally, when any predominant thought is brought forth there is always opposition. Those who oppose the recreative act choose to isolate themselves and become ascetics. This is their choice, because primarily they do not feel responsible for bringing new life from the old.

Many of these so-called "masters" that have isolated themselves from society are fakes. They are escapists. They are looking for a way out of the responsibilities of life. They have no reverence toward anything, although they would present a "front" to make others believe that they are sacred people.

Throughout the universe, birth is a privilege of parents. It is the proof manifest that they are qualified to recreate with the Creator.

Recreation is the eternal progression of creation. Science is the art of measuring the ever-changing progression. The sciences converted to the destruction of today will only result in a disaster that will be a lesson for the future.

THE COUNCIL OF SEVEN LIGHTS

O mortals cast in density of form, I center the Light to guide your way. My Light is not seen by those who observe only the density of figure.

Neither can I violate the Laws I have made in the Wisdom of My eternal ways. I cannot but stay at rest with you, hoping that the best will reach for Me, that I may bring your perception into the Light.

Man closes doors, man hides himself. He binds himself to possessions of dust, not realizing all is lost to him and lost to Me. For only by the progression of thee, do I progress. My parts are scattered throughout My boundless Being. I move in many ways to fashion My completeness. Each part shall find the resurrection in Me, though the time is recorded in the records lost in space. My eternity is only complete in the patience of Myself in thee.

And so I wait within, with the knowing that My beginnings never end.

O man, in the everchanging pattern of My thoughts I bring My creatures into being. In seeing motion all about, never doubt that I am there. For I am motion, change, and time, so that My rhyme of repetition may cycle all My parts.

Your eyes reach out to see the stars, not realizing each has stars within. Though sin may barricade your way to Me, change will be your sword to rend the veil and I shall hail you in your victory over self.

Though My time is naught to Me, time to you is meant to be a gauge to register progression in My ways.

THE COUNCIL OF SEVEN LIGHTS

Motion is the Me in thee, O man, to manifest a change, so that in time you may escape the rhyme of rebirth repetitions and be timelessly the peaceful thought of Me—eternally.

INDEX

A

"A" line, 21, 33, 34
  as agent of balance, 26
  discarge of, 55
  is God's right hand, 21
  seeks impregnation, 55
  male, projective polarity, 21, 24
  number, 24
  speed of, 24, 25, 53
  "Us", 26

Adamic, 15, 18
  colony, 16, 120
  Confederation, 31
  Man, 15, 31
  Race, 15, 16, 37, 115, 118
  story of Adam, 17

Angels, 80, 83, 85, 89, 112, 130
  in Bible, 84
  creation, 84
  Man; are, 83, 84

Animal, 18, 31, 37, 39
  body, 18, 75, 135
  Man, 32
  mating with, 17, 31
  Race of Eve, 17, 18
  Second Density; in the, 31

Arc, 30, 95
  matter; of, 84
  of "Noe", 39, 40
  of "Spae", 31, 40

Ark, 39
  Noah's, 31
  size of, 39

Atmosphere, 54, 55, 93, 94, 98
  as a bearing, 55, 105
  breathable, 18
  is a brush, 55
  clouds, 110
  as a field, 55
  heat, 55, 101
  humidity, 56, 110
  ionization of, 110
  negative; is, 44, 55, 56, 96, 108
  atomic radiation in our, 18, 56, 98, 108

Atom, 22, 24, 34, 73
  activation of, 33
  birth of, 21-23
  cluster of consciousness, 73
  core, 44
  cracking of, 23
  element, 21, 23, 73
  energy, 20, 57
  isotopes, 20
  pressure, 23

Aurora, 25, 94

Aura, 75, 87
  spirit body; is, 86
  vibration of, 88

Axis, 58, 66, 107, 108
  polar, 108

B

"B" line, 21, 33, 34, 71
  is agent of balance, 26
  seeks fecundation, 55
  female, receptive polarity, 21, 24, 71
  is God's left hand, 21
  number, 24
  speed, 24, 25, 53
  "Us", 26

Balance, 19, 34, 37, 55, 56,

INDEX

64, 74, 76, 77, 97
rhythmic, 34
unbalance, 19, 47, 64, 76, 108

Being, 62, 65-67, 75, 137, 138
existence in space, 62
God; is, 67

Blocks,
Great Pyramid; of, 116

Blood, 136
crossed, 17
flow, 135

Body, 33, 34, 51, 57, 58, 74, 100, 131, 135, 138
"A" and "B" lines through 33
activity, 34
animal, 18, 86, 102, 107, 119, 120, 135, 136
celestial, 50
cells, 33
energy, 57
motion; in, 44
of Reality, 18, 66, 75, 136
spirit, 86
square, 44

Bombs
atomic, 17, 18, 20, 43, 98, 107
Hydrogen, 17, 98, 107-109

C

Cataclysm, 31
coming, 32, 90, 118

Cell
body, 33
center, 136
control master, 136, 137
changing of every 7 and 28 years, 137
essence of form, 136
master, 75, 136, 137
vegetation; in, 36

Church
beginnings, 141
buildings, 141
Seven, 112

Consciousness, 33, 73-75, 137, 138, 140
is dormant, 9
expansion of, 138
individual, 12
of Third Density, 37

Core, 25, 26, 93, 116
atomic, 44
axis, 107
positive polarity, 55, 93, 107
square, 44

Creation, 73, 141
is evolving, 15
existence since the, 12
finished, 16
original, 15
people; of, 16
principle of, 11
progression of, 29, 142

Creator, 16, 29, 63, 83, 93, 129, 132, 139, 142
at rest, 19
Thoughts, 29, 30

Cross; Maltese, 58

Crust, 26, 93, 94, 98, 106
as commutator, 55
female, negative polarity,

146

INDEX

25, 55, 93, 96, 104
 ruptures of, 93

Crystal, 44
 animal, 136
 battery, 86, 87
 blood stream; in, 135, 136
 neutral, 135
 polarized, 135
 records in, 136
 vegetable, 136

Cycle, 35, 37, 38, 65
 of "Dust to Dust", 35
 Major (12), 30, 38
 Master (12), 30, 38
 Minor (12), 30, 38
 morning, 101
 of Precession of Equinox, 38
 quarterly, 98
 of rebirth, 15
 of repetition, 88
 2100 year, 38
 26,000 year, 38

D

Density, 24, 29, 35, 132, 140
 alternate polarity, 32
 between, 30
 elements; of, 23
 of emergence, 37
 First, 30, 35-37, 39
 Fourth, 30-32, 37
 as grades, 29, 132
 as levels, 29
 Master cycle, 30
 of quantity, 25
 Second, 30, 31, 37
 Third, 29-32, 37
 Thirteenth, 24
 twelve, 30

Dimension, 35, 66, 87, 115, 118, 140
 and Density, 32
 Fourth, 85
 measurements; as, 32

E

Earth, 11, 12, 18, 22, 30, 52, 54, 111
 atmosphere of, 55, 94, 104, 105
 as a battery, 55, 93, 99
 core of, 25, 26, 93, 104, 106
 diameter, 22
 First Density on, 30, 36
 force field of, 52, 54, 55, 94, 99, 100, 103, 131
 as a generator, 55, 99
 as a gyroscope, 107

Moon's effect on, 99
 as a motor, 55, 99
 is negative, 56, 74, 95, 97, 100, 116
 orbit, 56, 63, 105
 people, 15, 17, 29, 31, 40, 89
 poles, 31, 56, 90
 has a positive force field, 54, 100, 103, 111
 rotation, 22, 30, 39, 52, 56, 63, 66, 106, 121, 129
 seven levels around the, 112
 speed of, 52
 stopped by, 52
 Sun; never part of, 105
 surface, 36, 51, 74-76, 90
 tides, 99, 103
 tilt, 97
 "time" field, 51, 52

INDEX

Earthquake
 Bible; in, 30, 38
 fault, 93
 increase of, 107
 time of, 38

Electricity
 cause of, 100, 104, 109
 "piezo", 86, 87
 static, 58, 86

Electron, 23, 94
 "B" particles are, 21
 discharge of, 24

Energy, 43, 57, 105
 atomic, 20, 57
 conversion of, 50
 female, 71
 matter; is, 19, 50, 53
 Mind; directed by, 43
 negative, 56
 positive, 56
 primary, 52, 53, 119
 unbalanced, 19

Equator, 94, 96, 116
 Earth; of, 95
 land south or north of, 56
 magnetic, 51

Eve, 16-18
 extinct; became, 31
 Race of, 17, 31
 story of, 16, 17

F

Female, 35, 36, 137, 141
 energy, 71
 flight of, 24
 polarity, 21, 24, 71
Flesh, 66, 136, 140
 animal, 31

body, 12, 66
 eating of, 37

Field, 74-76
 auric, 75
 force, 54, 88, 103, 116
 negative, 23, 52, 53, 111
 oscillates, 103
 "time", 51, 109

Force, 29, 84
 "angle of attack", 34
 attractive, 104
 eternal, 120
 Light, 24
 lines of, 33, 34, 52, 56, 74
 repelling, 104
 soul, 75
 unbalanced, 36

Frequency, 22, 37, 58, 74, 75, 88, 131, 136
 animal's, 75
 determines elemental density, 23

Fusion
 atmosphere; in negative, 56, 98, 108
 between photosphere and actisphere, 44

G

"G" line, 21, 22, 33, 136
 God; symbol of, 21
 inrush of, 23
 as insulation, 22, 25
 intelligence; is, 22
 light, 22, 23, 25
 motion of, 22
 "Us", 26

Genesis, 83
 1:1, 15

INDEX

1:11, 12, 17
1:21, 22, 17
1:26, 26
1:27, 15
1:28, 16
2:1, 16
2:2, 3, 16
2:18, 16
2:21, 22, 16
3:1-7, 17
4:1, 17
chapter 5, 120
7:20, 39
chapter 10, 40
16:7, 84

God, 11, 12, 16, 21, 37, 43
  67, 93
  beginning of creation, 15
  finished creation, 16, 127
  Image, 67, 73, 128
  is Infinite Being, 11, 67,
    128
  instruments, 15, 71
  It, 128, 139
  Law, 17
  Lord, 16
  manifestations of, 11

  Mind, 67
  as Peace, 19
  power, 121, 128
  scientifically, 140
  son of, 17, 38, 118
  understanding of, 12
  as Wisdom, 24

Gravity, 75, 118
  Earth's, 51, 94
  lines of force causes, 55
  resistance pressure; is, 55,
    59
  within force fields, 100

H

Ham, 40
  black people, 40
  landed, 40
  Race of, 40

Heat, 101, 103
  cause of, 34, 55, 95, 96,
    100
  contraction, 100
  expansion, 100
  frictional, 54, 107
  resistance, 102, 108

Hemisphere, 51, 97
  negative Northern, 95-97,
    103
  positive Southern, 95, 97,
    103, 108

Human, 11, 17, 18, 29, 31,
  37, 40, 58, 75, 88, 100
  120, 131
  extinction of, 32
  Intelligence, 40
  Man becomes, 17
  reproduction, 31
  tendencies, 18, 31
  vortices, 75

I

Infinity, 21, 64, 65
  three aspects of, 65

Influence, 34
  atmospheric, 33
  electronic, 33
  metallic objects; of, 33
  negative, 57
  people, 33
  planets, 33

INDEX

Insulation, 58, 71, 93
  "G" lines as, 23, 24
  layers of, 29, 93, 104
  time as, 53

Intelligence, 9, 36, 47, 62, 64, 74, 128
  balanced, 19, 47
  Creative, Infinite, 22, 29, 47, 73, 93, 126
  fulcrum of, 21
  "G" light is, 22
  layers of, 23
  manifested, 63
  organized, 9
  thought is image of, 29, 63

J

Japheth, 40
  landed, 40
  Race of, 40
  yellow people, 40

Jesus, 19
  birth, 111
  disciples, 126
  formula used by, 126
  his people, 118
  intuition, 118
  journey, 118
  miracles, 87, 126
  neutral, 19
  Teacher, Savior, Son of God, 38, 89
  voice of God to, 124
  "Word", 128

K

King's Chamber, 118
  open tomb in, 119
  regenerative powers, 119

L

Law, 9, 34, 40, 58, 84, 88, 127, 132
  God's, 17
  of gravity, 75
  reaction; of, 20
  violation of God's, 71

Life, 12, 35, 64, 66, 78
  animal, 17
  essence of, 35, 64
  Eternal, Infinite, 12, 64, 120
  First Density, 35
  forms of, 15, 18, 37, 56, 65, 75
  Light; is, 139
  lines, 74
  long, secret of, 137
  manifesting of, 35, 64-66, 127, 140
  space; in, 62, 64
  span, 12, 63, 120, 121
  Staff of, 36, 140
  spiral of, 35
  understood by Intelligence 62

Light, 86, 132
  absorption by negative bodies, 48
  bending of, 46, 87
  emission by positive bodies, 47, 99
  energy, 56-58
  oppositely charged, 23, 53, 76, 97, 102, 129
  primary, 46, 47, 57, 58
  reflection, 85, 100
  secondary, 47, 49, 101
  Seven, 112
  speed, 46, 53
  staff of, 140

INDEX

stars; from, 48
Still, One, 93
traveling, 48
warp, 46
wave length, 85

Luke, St.
17:35, 36, 88
17:37, 89
21:36, 90
24:13, 21, 87
24:31, 87
24:36-39, 87

M

Magnet, magnetism, 44, 59
cause, 56, 100, 104, 109
compass, 83, 105
conductor of polarity, 57
cutting of a, 36, 86
declination, 108
equator, 51
month, 129
on surface of Earth, 51, 104, 107
poles, 56, 57, 105, 107
is a secondary force, 104
shifting of poles, 107
speed of, 53
vortex, 93

Man, 20, 37, 57, 67, 129
Adamic Race of, 17, 127
angels are, 84
animal, 32
creation, 15, 73, 83, 127
doings, 29
mating of, 17, 141

Materialization, 131
of angels or space people, 130, 131

Matter, 10, 19, 52, 63, 93
conversion of, 50
digestion of, 66
energy; is condensed, 19, 50, 52
energy released from, 43
is inert, 68, 75
motion, 63, 105

Metal
conductors, 34
effect on sleep, 34

Mind, 9, 43, 48, 52, 64, 67, 77, 119, 137, 139, 140
creations, 67, 131
directs energy, 43
God; of, 67, 140
narrow, 15
neutral, 43
penetration of, 9, 43, 64

Mineral
cubic, 44
crystallized, 44
polarity, 44

Moon, 99, 101
on crops and people; effects, 33
"New Jerusalem", 110
orbit and speed, 101, 103
polarity, 100, 101
positive, 110
"Shanchea", 110
tides, 33, 103

Motion, 34, 37, 47, 53, 56, 57, 59, 63-65, 127, 136
circular, 34
manifesting, 19, 58, 63, 140
perpetual, 24
points of least, 46

INDEX

in Second Density, 37
speed of, 25
wave, 24

N

Negative, 23-25, 35, 36, 44,
  48, 52, 55, 57, 58, 71,
  94, 96, 102, 105, 111
body has positive force
  field, 100
body rotates counter-
  clockwise, 55, 71
currents, 52, 53, 129
fields, 23, 52, 53, 111
quarter, 102

Noah, 39
  Ark, 31
  God; walked with, 38
  sons, 40

Noe (arc of), 39
  animals in, 39, 40
  Earth flip in, 39
  flood in, 39

O

Obsidian
  fluid glass, 600 miles
    thick, 93, 107
Orbit, 53, 56, 57, 94
  diameters, 56
  Earth's, 52
  elliptical, 56, 97

P

People, 40, 63, 83
  black, 40
  creation of, 16
  Earth's, 29
  negative, 102

positive, 102
144,000, 89
"saved", 89
Space, 31, 37, 83, 85, 89,
  115, 130
white, 40
yellow, 40

Pharaohs, 115, 119
  mummification of, 119
  restored to life, 119

Planet, 31, 51, 52, 55, 57,
  83, 94, 97
  atomic fission and fusion
    on, 20
  "housecleaning", 37, 38
  influences, 33
  interruption of light lines,
    33, 56
  is living, 65
  movement of, 94
  rebalancing, 30, 56, 57, 89
  has self-generated
    magnetic field, 54

Pole, polarity, 25, 94, 105
  axis, 108
  balance of, 51, 56, 75, 110
  change of, 97, 107
  Densities; of, 32
  negative receptive, 108
  neutral, 75
  new, 30, 56, 89
  North, 25, 105, 108
  opposite, 23, 53, 56, 76,
    97, 102, 129
  positive projective, 102,
    108
  predominance, 48, 97, 102
  repelling, 78
  South, 25, 108
  Sun; of, 46

INDEX

unbalanced, 46
zero, 76

Positive, 35, 36, 46-48, 52, 55-57, 93, 98, 102, 108, 111, 118, 138
 body has negative force field, 100
 body rotates clockwise, 55, 71
 lines, 25, 52, 56, 95, 96, 129
 quarter (spring), 94, 101
 vortex, 106, 116

Principle, 9, 54
 creative, 20
 of cyclotron, 118
 of fountain of youth, 121
 One, 11, 21, 71
 of primary energy, 119
 of saucer, 82
 of Sun, 20
 of Wheel of Life, 35

Proton, 44
 is atomic nucleus, 21
 discharge of, 24
 is positive, 23
Pyramid, Great, 115, 119
 building of, 116
 capstone of, 116
 definition of, 115
 location of, 116
 missing courses, 118
 power principle, 115, 118
 weight of, 116

Q

Quarter, Active (Summer), 95, 102, 104
 hottest part of day; and season, 95, 101

Quarter, Negative (Fall), 102, 104

Quarter, Positive (Spring), 94, 95, 101, 104, 129

Quarter, Rest (Winter), 95, 102
 balancing of forces in, 96, 97
 cooling off, 102
 death and low resistance, 98, 102
 midnight to 6 A.M., 102
 movement of Universe in, 97

R

Race, 40
 Adamic, Man, 18, 127
 Animal, Eve, 18
 Ham, 40
 Japheth, 40
 Shem, 40

Reincarnation, 32, 71, 73
 misnomer, 12, 73
 proof of, 127
Rejuvenation, 119, 121
 possible for 50 to 80 year, 121

Religion, 10, 11, 24
 is art of living, 11
 many roads of, 11

Revelations
 earthquake in, 30, 38
 1:20, 112
 chapter 2, 112
 chapter 3, 112
 5:11, 112
 21:10, 110

INDEX

21:11, 112
21:16, 111

Rotate, rotation, 25, 46, 57, 93, 94
  corners of Sun, 44, 46
  Densities; of, 32
  speed of, 39, 56

S

Sex, 77
  Bible; in, 142
  relation to religion, 141
  throughout history, 141, 142

Shem, 40
  landed, 40
  Race, 40
  white people, 40

Ship, 118
  "Earthchild", 111
  entering, 88
  "New Jerusalem", 110
  nullifier, 18
  positive, square, star body, 111
  scout, 86
  "Shanchea", 111, 112
  "Star of Bethlehem", 111
  vortex, 83

Solar
  emanation, 57
  system, 15, 21, 29, 30, 32, 37, 51, 52, 65, 115
  Tongue, 111
  vortex, 116

Space, 32, 43, 51, 53, 57, 62, 64-67, 94, 97
  is balanced cubes, 47
  is composed of Life, Time,
    Being, and Intelligence, 19, 47, 62, 67, 74
  drebis, 54
  people, 31, 37, 85, 89, 100 111, 112, 115, 124, 130, 131

Space craft, 16, 20, 38, 53, 54, 81, 84, 111
  contacts, 85, 89
  control, 52
  force field, 54, 88, 100
  humming noise of, 54
  silent travel, 54
  size of, 82
  skipping, 54
  speed of, 54
  "vailx", 116

Spae (arc of), 40
  cataclysm in, 31
  landing in, 40

Species, 23, 35, 74

Sphere
  negative actisphere, 44, 47, 49
  positive photosphere, 44, 47
  is an unbalanced negative body, 48

Spiral, 25, 36
  apex of, 32
  Densities are, 32
  Eternal, 35
  of Life, 35

Spirit, 12, 26, 37, 75, 77, 86, 88, 140
  Creative, 73, 132, 140
  matter; and, 18, 19
  recognition of, 37

INDEX

Sun, 43, 44, 93, 94, 97, 103, 105
  actisphere, 44, 49
  cubic body in, 44, 46
  energy, 43
  equator, 46
  field vortex, 49, 55, 95-97
  negative half, 46
  operation, 20
  path on Earth, 95
  planet; is an evolved, 43
  poles, 46
  positive polarity, 36, 46, 55, 95, 99, 101, 105, 112
  rotation, 44, 46, 47
  spots, 44, 47
  "time" field, 51
  positive vortex, 95

T

Temperature
  cause of, 100
  in First Density, 30
  in Fourth Density, 32
  germination, 30, 56
  increase of, 107
  lowering of, 98, 107
  in Second Density, 31, 39
  in Third Density, 31
  of 90° F., 32
  of 98.6° F. 31
  of 104° F., 31
  of 110° F., 30

Thought, 9, 52, 76, 126, 131
  is activating force, 29, 126, 130
  Creative, 29, 67, 129
  Image of Intelligence, 29, 63
  motion is energy, 63, 65
  power, 10, 124, 126
  reception, 9, 12, 124, 125
  "Tele", 82
  transference, 81
  transmission, 9

Thought communication, 9, 83, 86, 124
  accomplishment of, 9
  blanking of mind needed, 125
  concentration, use of, 125, 129
  dormant on Earth, 124
  increasing power of, 125
  instrumentation, use of, 124
  interruption of, 124
  power formula for, 126, 128
  power of 1, 2, 3, 4, and 12, 124-126
  positive polarity, 127-129
  release of, 125, 129

Tide, 103
  age, 103
  cause, 103
  four, 103
  lag, 104

Time, 65, 66
  Absolute, 32, 62
  goes backward, 32
  ceases, 51
  changes in, 34, 64
  divisions of, 120
  exists in space, 62
  field, 51, 52, 109
  goes forward, 32
  is measurable, 62, 65
  passage through, 53, 67
  phasing of, 32
  planetary, 38

is repetition, 65
is a separator, 52
staying in, 51
stillness of, 53
understanding of, 62

U

Universe, 57, 65, 94, 126, 129, 142
is expanding, 43
forces, 129
"flowers", 30
is Infinite, 11
Law, 83, 88, 115, 127, 132
of light, 132

V

Vibration, 22, 32, 88, 124, 131, 132
of body, 88, 131
increasing, 32

Vision, 87, 138
negative, limited, physical, 48, 58, 85, 87, 130, 139
sees reflected positive light, 49
sees negative light reflected from positive body, 49

Vortex, 55, 74-78, 105, 118
discharge, 78
helical, 105
human, negative, 75, 77
human, positive, 75, 77
individual, 78
leakage of, 77
magnetic on Earth, 93
physical, 76
positive solar, 95, 116
of Real You, 76
of ship, 83

W

Water, 33, 36, 39, 116
fifteen cubits deep, 39
firmament; in, 39
Life; of, 36
is negative, 36, 103, 108
witcher's twig, 36

Y

Year, 33
of 370 days, 32
9, 116
2100, 38
25,816, 115
25,825, 116
26,000, 38

Z

Zechariah
4:1, 80

www.ingramcontent.com/pod-product-compliance
Lightning Source LLC
Chambersburg PA
CBHW051941160426
43198CB00013B/2250